AF574715

MACRAMÉ

MACRAMÉ

Ann Stearns

With over 230 black-and-white illustrations and 8 pages of colour plates

DAVID & CHARLES
NEWTON ABBOT LONDON VANCOUVER

ARCO PUBLISHING COMPANY, INC
NEW YORK

This edition first published in 1975
in Great Britain by
David & Charles (Publishers) Limited,
Newton Abbot, Devon,
in the USA by
Arco Publishing Company, Inc.,
219 Park Avenue South,
New York, NY 10003
in Canada by
Douglas David & Charles Limited,
1875 Welch Street
North Vancouver BC

0 7153 6629 7 (Great Britain)
Arco Order Number 3669
LCCCN 74-25009

Second impression 1976
Third impression 1978

Printed photolitho in Great Britain
by Ebenezer Baylis & Son Limited
The Trinity Press, Worcester, and London

CONTENTS

ACKNOWLEDGEMENTS

I am indebted to Maureen Hobbs, Susan Ball, Ann Andrew, Margaret Hammond, and Margaret Morley, students who carried out the macramé designs on pages 30, 41, 58, 61 and 73; and to Betty Henderson whose dress appears on page 54.

My husband Bryan Stearns took the photographs for me and earns my grateful thanks for the help and encouragement he has given during the writing of this book.

AS
Horton-cum-Studley

INTRODUCTION

During the last few years a number of books have appeared which provide readers with a broad view of the uses and methods of macramé work. The intention of this book is to demonstrate to the macramé worker the application of this ancient craft to fashion.

The illustrations range widely from accessories which can be easily and quickly made by a beginner, for whom step by step instructions are provided, to more advanced designs which, while employing the same basic knotting techniques, nevertheless require more experience and skill.

The development of expertise will enable many readers to reproduce the designs shown in this book. It is the author's ambition to encourage experimentation, as the production of unique designs is much more rewarding than copying patterns already worked.

One of the great attractions of the craft of macramé is the small amount of equipment required. Practically everything can be obtained easily and cheaply. Indeed, the simplest equipment is a length of string and a chair back.

The sort of work which can be produced varies enormously. On one hand, a complicated and sophisticated pair of ear rings, illustrated below, has been made from aluminium passing twist, while on the other, a very simple belt made from farmer's baler twine has been produced. Each has its own separate appeal.

The attraction of macramé is universal. Traditionally, the sailor has been the expert in decorative knotting, in many respects closely allied to macramé work. The craft is easily learned by young and old; failing eyesight is no special disadvantage as touch plays an important part in the work.

A belt made in natural coloured farmer's baler twine. Two large wood rings and a plaited sinnet form the tie fastening

(Left)
A pair of ear rings made in silver aluminium passing twist

EQUIPMENT AND MATERIALS

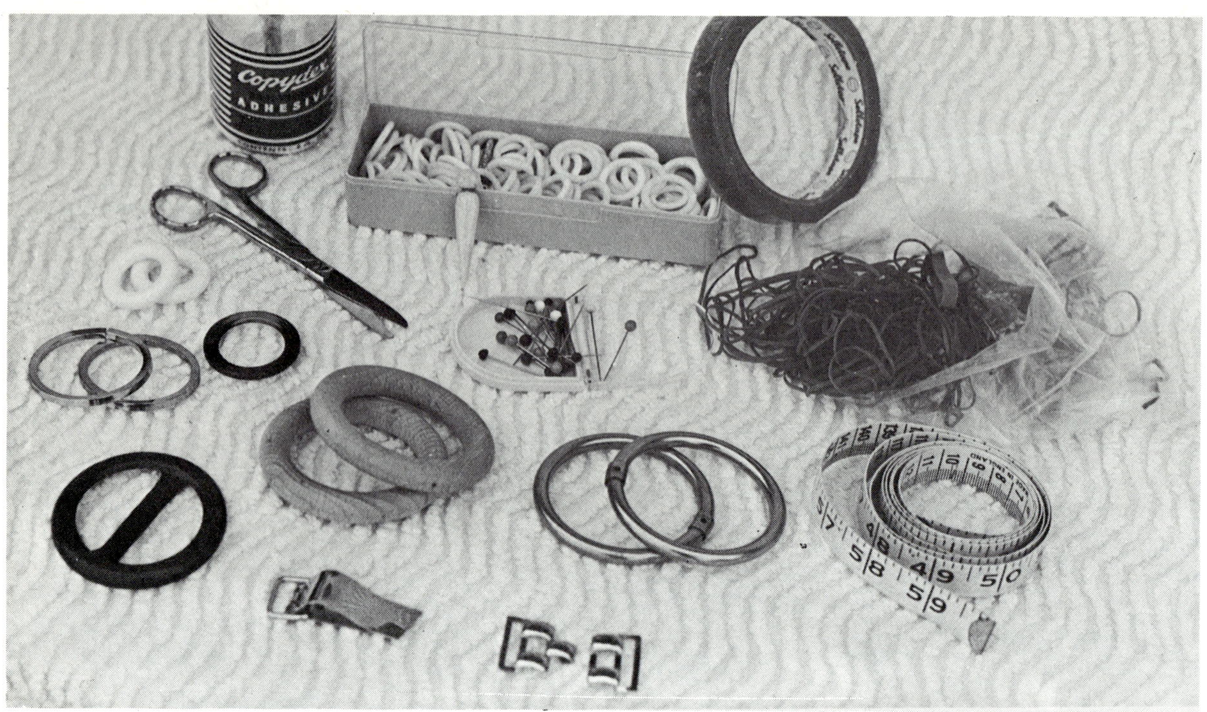

One of the principle attractions of macramé is the small amount of equipment required and the ease with which it can be acquired. The photograph above illustrates some of the tools used for knotting. However, many of the items, such as the rings and buckles, are really extras required only for the job in hand.

The main essential is a firm surface on which to work. Commercial macramé boards are available from handicraft suppliers, but little skill is required to make one. At the outset, the setting up of a tight foundation cord is important. This can be achieved by anchoring the two ends of a piece of cord between drawer handles, a chair back, two nails in a piece of hard board or, for mobility, on a work board. A board of this type is illustrated here; it is made from a piece of 6- or 8-ply wood about 40cm × 30cm, covered securely with sheeting or towelling. A bull-dog clip is useful to hold the cover in place at the top of the board.

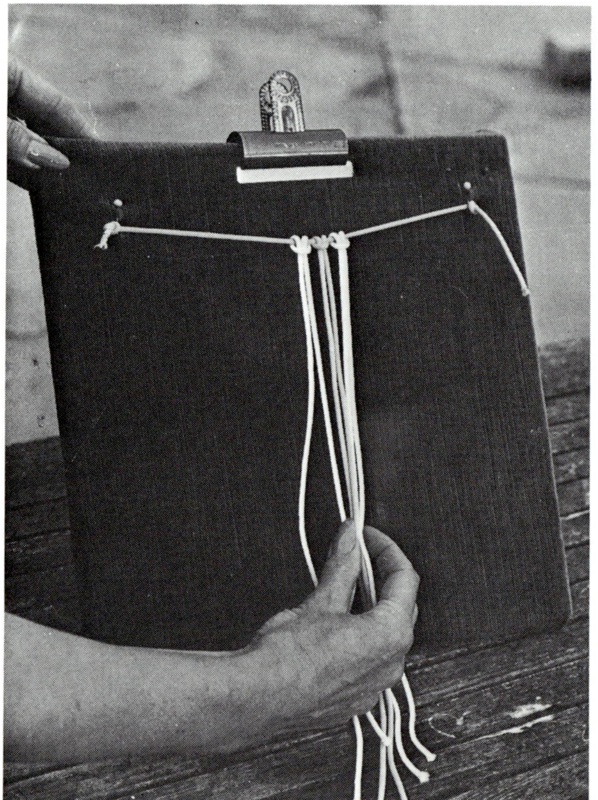

G-cramps screwed to a wooden base also give a secure foundation. The photograph above shows work in progress on such a board. When making certain articles, for example a bag, the actual handles will form the foundation cord and the knotting is worked straight on to the frame of the bag handle. The bag frame is then weighted or tied down to a firm surface before the knotting is started. If the design is simple, no work board is required.

Instead of a rigid work board, a useful alternative is a working pad or cushion, made by placing rubber foam on a firm wooden base and then covering the whole very tightly with two or three pieces of strong calico. The advantage of this is that pins to hold the work in place can easily be inserted and adjusted.

The other pieces of useful equipment are
glass headed pins
crochet hooks
adhesive tape
rubber based adhesive
selection of canvas sewing needles
tape measure and/or ruler
elastic bands
rat tail files (for enlarging bead holes)
dyes
selection of bought commercial beads or handmade beads.

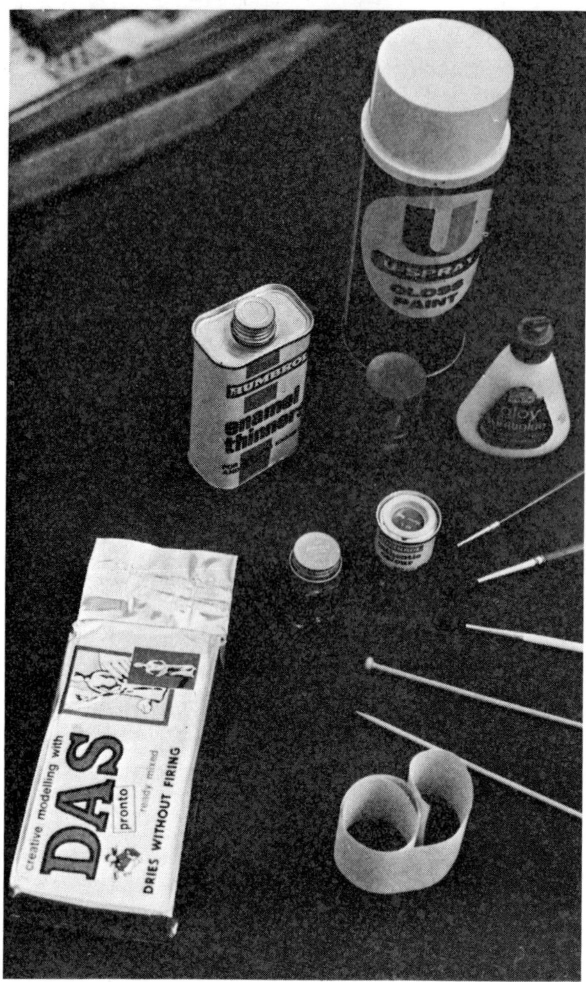

The various materials and equipment used for making the clay beads and paper beads which are used in some of the designs in this book

Some of the yarns used in work described in this book

The choice of material is of great importance as it essentially governs the scale of the design.

When making a piece of macramé for a dress decoration it is of course important that it should be appropriate for the fabric, and it is wise to work a trial piece and pin the work to the garment. Stand back to judge the effect; often, a trim which looks attractive in isolation appears disappointing when attached to the material. Any cord, yarn or thread can be used for macramé work. Fabric rouleau cords in the same or contrasting materials are suitable for knotting. Cords made by twisting finer threads together, rug wool, crochet yarns and lurex threads all make excellent materials for work.

Particularly successful results can be obtained by using piping cord which is available in varying thicknesses. This cord may be dyed to the exact colour required, although it must be washed first if the cord is not being dyed as it tends to shrink. Searching local shops and open markets often proves most rewarding as the success of a design depends so much on the novelty of the materials used.

BASIC KNOTS

HALF KNOT OR MACRAMÉ KNOT

All macramé is based on the variation of two simple knots—the square or flat knot and the half hitch. All designs are developed from these knots.

The square knot is formed from the half knot (also called the macramé knot) and it is necessary to understand its formation.

Place and secure an anchoring cord across the work board and loop on two halved cords. Tie an overhand knot on the left hand cord and bring this across and over two and under one cord.

Take the right hand cord over and behind the knotted cord, then under the middle two cords and over the left hand cord. This completes the half knot.

Repeat the half knot, but particularly note that the cords have changed sides—the cord with the knot tied in it travels behind this time.

The third half knot has now been tied with the knotted cord travelling over the two centre cords.

Here is a photograph of a completed run of identical half knots, called a Bannister bar. It will be noted that the two centre cords in this series always remain passive, the outside cords only forming the tie, which is worked alternately from side to side.

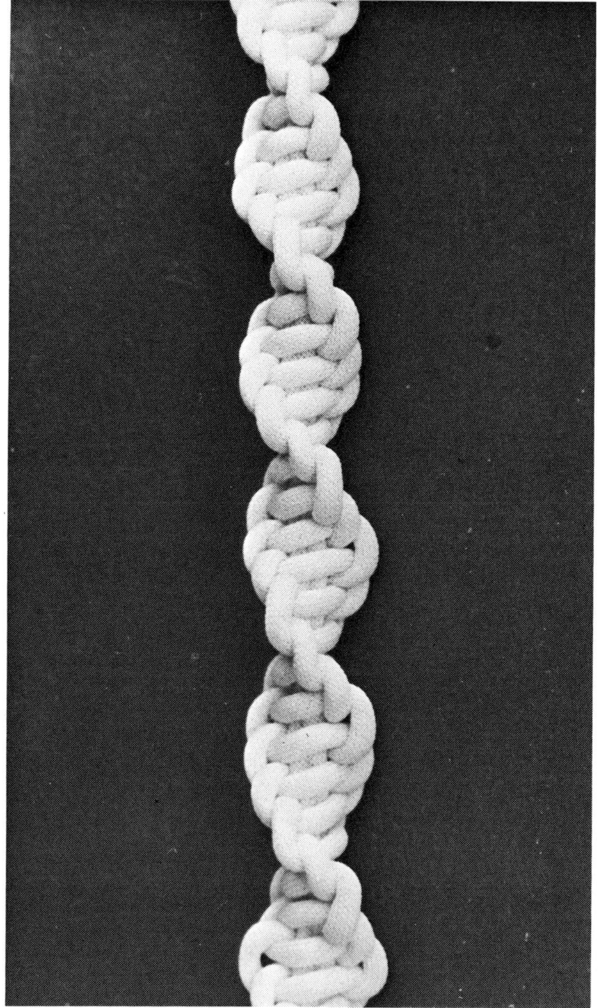

SQUARE KNOT OR FLAT KNOT

The square knot consists of two knots, the first of which is the half knot as illustrated on pp. 11-12.

The second part is formed by taking the knotted cord and bringing it across the two centre cords and behind the left hand cord.

Now take the left hand cord over the knotted and UNDER the two centre cords and over the right hand cord.

You have now completed one square knot.

The first half of the next square knot being worked.

Throughout the run, only the outside cords are tied and the knotted cord always passes OVER the centre cords.

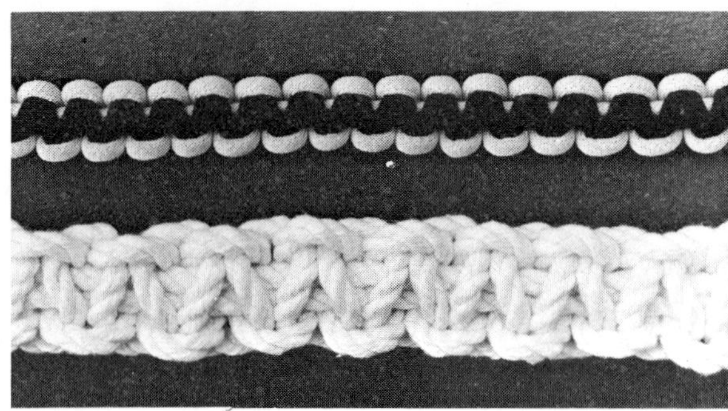

A run of square knots is called a Solomon bar. In the photograph, two pieces of square knots are shown. One piece has been worked in two colours.

Fabric in square knots worked in pairs. Each new row divides the cords from the knot above for the next square knot.

This run of square knots has incorporated a picot and an overhand knot. These are worked on the two outside cords. The knots are then tightened on the centre cords forming the picot.

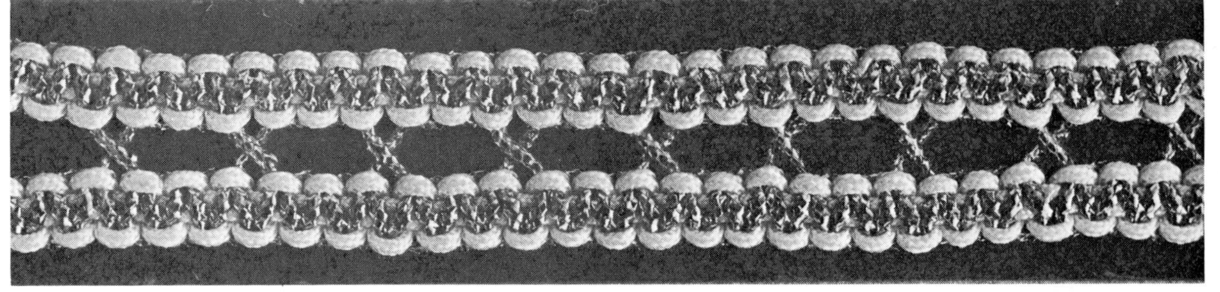

Two rows of square knots joined together by a crossover design of the centre cords.

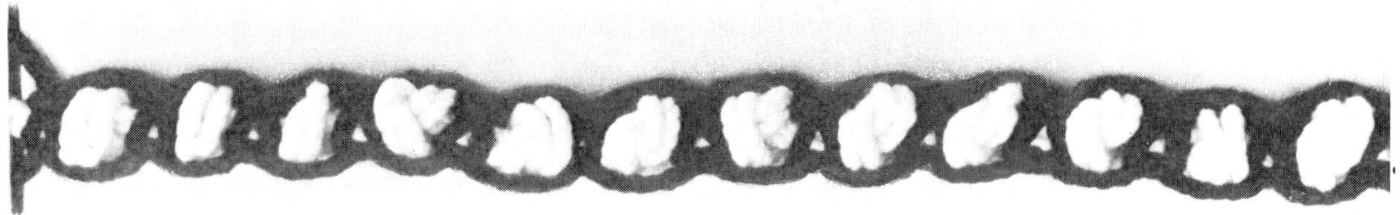

A run of square knots divided by an overhand knot worked with the centre cords. Two colours were used for this braid.

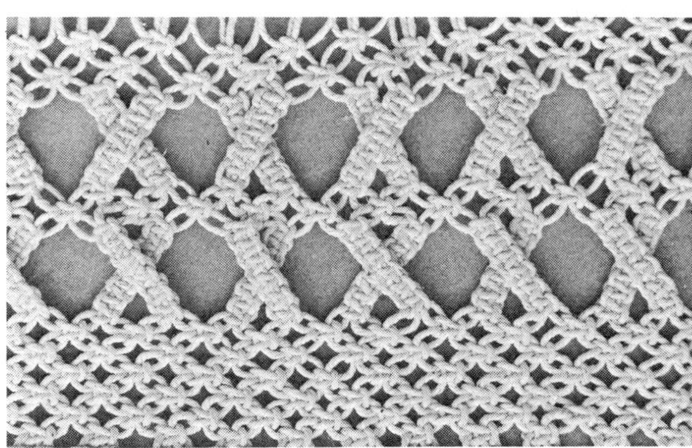

A crossover design worked in square knots. A single row of square knots holds and joins the crossover in place.

A wider braid worked in square knots. A silver lurex cord and pink cotton yarn were used for this braid.

HALF HITCH

The half hitch, when worked in pairs (double half hitch), is the knot used to form cording. Practise the single loop of the half hitch (also called the tatting knot) as shown in the centre of the photograph below. The right hand cord forms the core and the left hand cord the knot. When several knots have been worked in this way the working cord begins to twist around the centre cord. This is shown on the runs on either side.

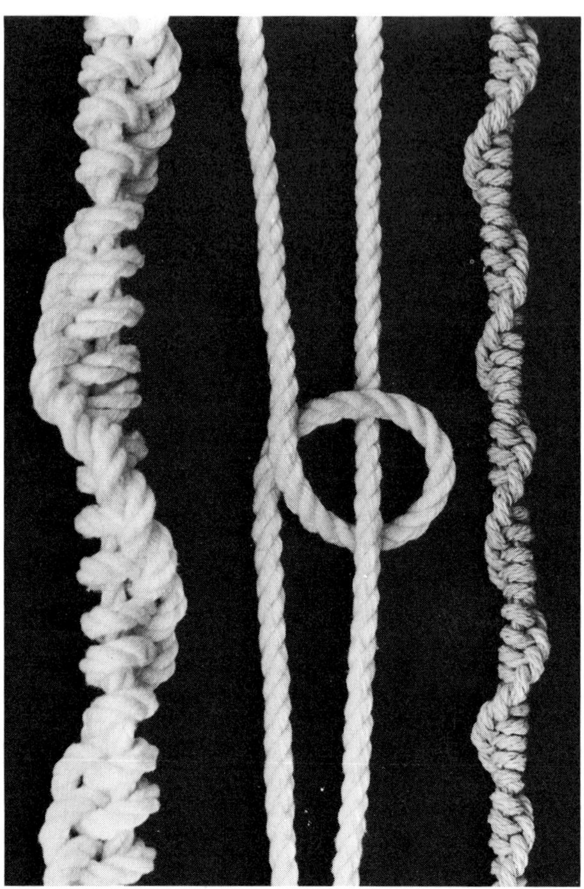

ALTERNATE HALF HITCH

Sailors call this a see-saw knot. In the photograph left the half hitch is worked left over right, but the knot can also be worked right over left. If the two knots are worked alternately, a chain is made. The centre of the photograph below demonstrates this knot. The completed chain is illustrated on either side. The knot can look attractive when made in interesting colour combinations and is used in many macramé designs.

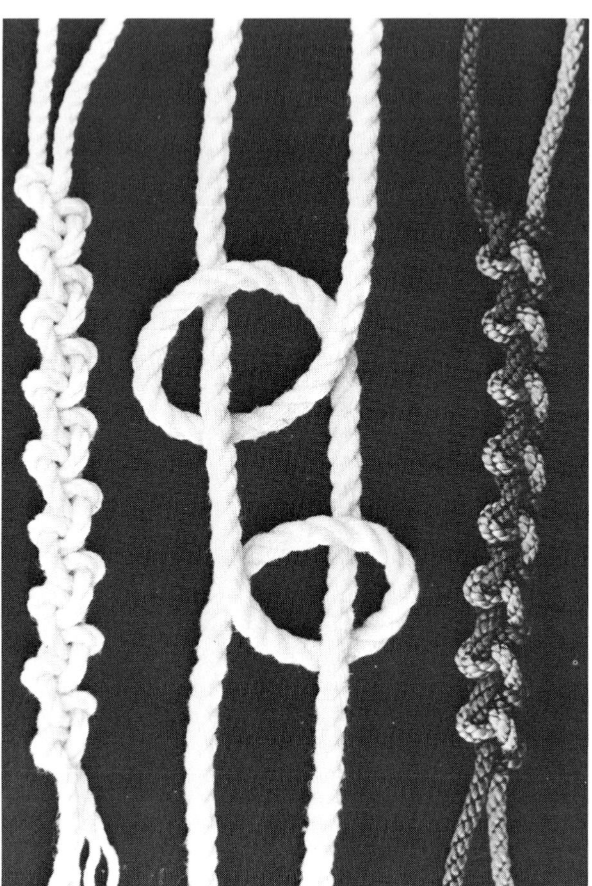

Boot with navy macramé fringe

A pair of boots

Gold braided and fringed evening dress

Bag in a circular design

A firm braid can be made by running two or more cords down the centre of the knots to form a core. Various colour combinations give interesting effects.

Tubular rayon cord is used in two colours to work half hitches over a double length of thick piping cord. The knotting is worked alternately from side to side. This is known as a Genoese bar.

Two braids are illustrated, made of the single half hitch knot. The top braid is worked over two centre cords. Two half hitches are worked from each side, first over one of the centre cords and then over both. This is repeated from each side. Two colours are used in this illustration.

The lower braid is similar; two lengths of braid are worked and then joined together down the centre.

a. The alternate half hitch or see-saw chain forms the majority of this braid. Cording and square knots are also used in this braid.

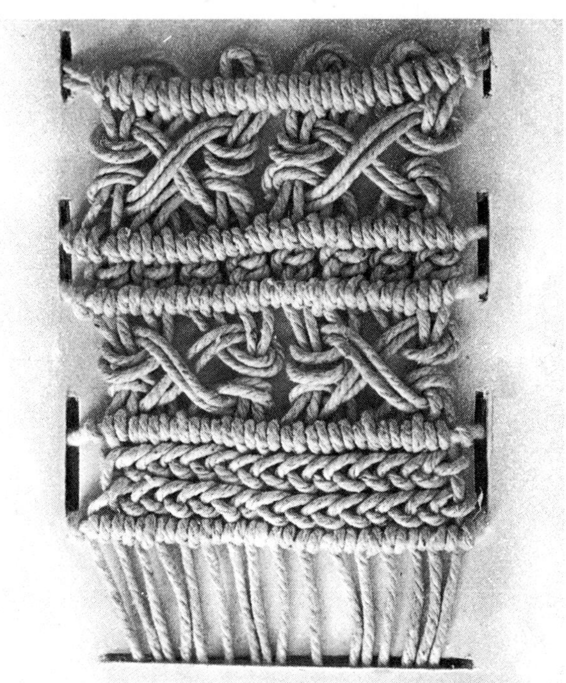

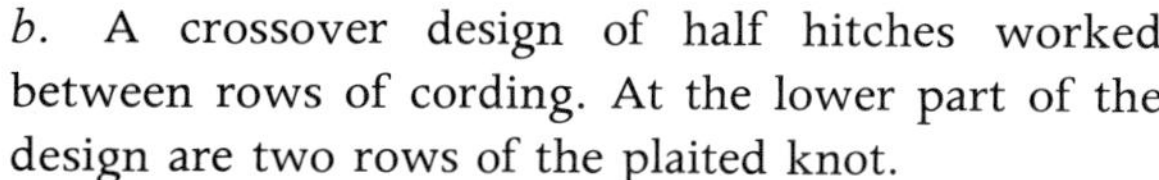

b. A crossover design of half hitches worked between rows of cording. At the lower part of the design are two rows of the plaited knot.

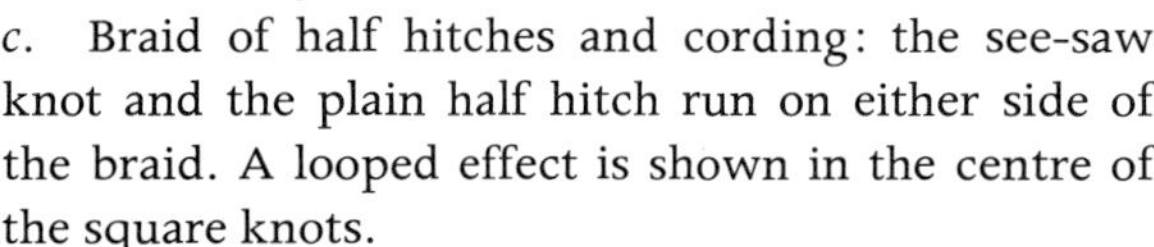

c. Braid of half hitches and cording: the see-saw knot and the plain half hitch run on either side of the braid. A looped effect is shown in the centre of the square knots.

DOUBLE HALF HITCH

The double half hitch, when worked with several cords, is known as cording, and this forms a great part of macramé work.

To practise cording worked in double half hitches, loop several cords on to a foundation cord which is securely held taut.

Take the left hand cord, which becomes the leader, and place it horizontally over the remaining cords. The leader must be held taut. The second cord forms the double half hitch on the leader.

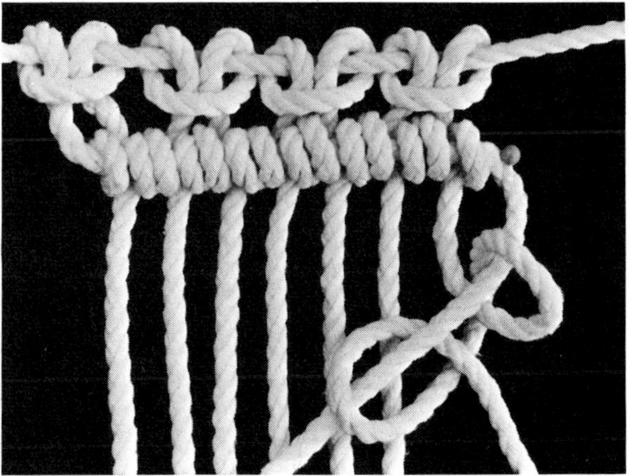

Each subsequent cord is then worked in the same way across the leader. When all the cords have been worked, the leader is secured, turned back over the working cords, and the process repeated.

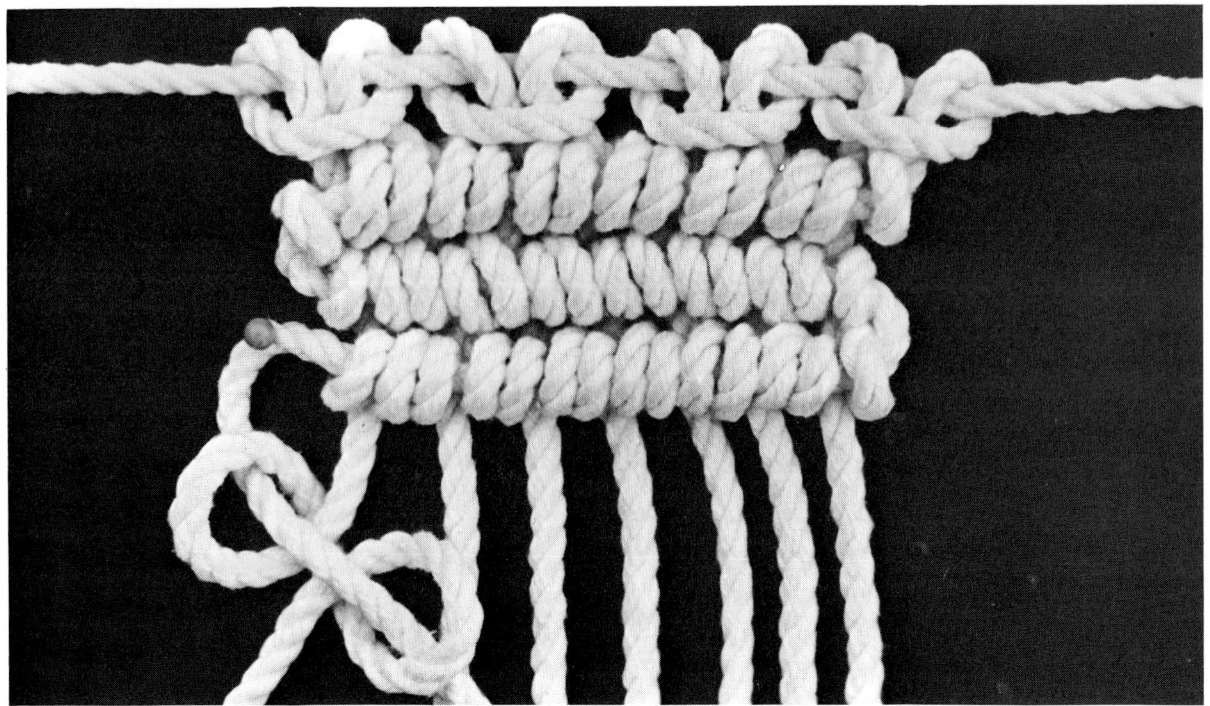

Three complete rows have been worked and a fourth started.

The cord forming the leader can be a separate cord introduced into the work and may be placed in any direction, ie horizontally or vertically.

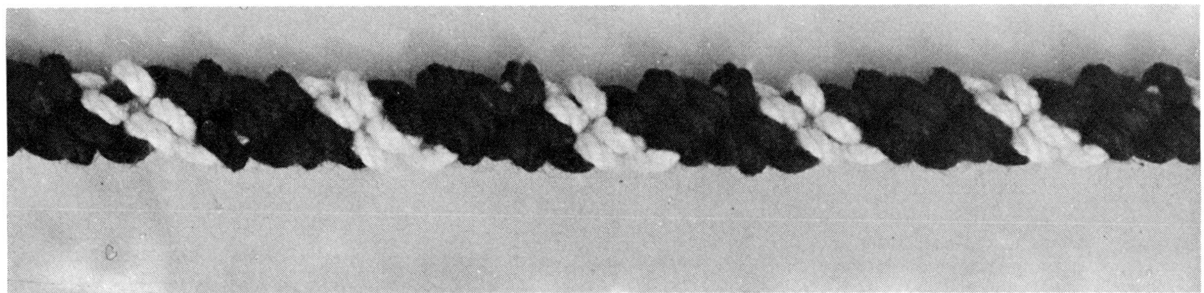

a. Cording worked diagonally in two colours.
b. Diagonal cording using the same leader continuously. The leader is held towards the left and then the right as required.

Interesting braids can be made using cording as the basis of the design. Beads can be added to emphasise the colour of the outfit for which the braid is being made.

a. White gimp is used for this braid. Silver and shocking pink beads are added during the knotting process.

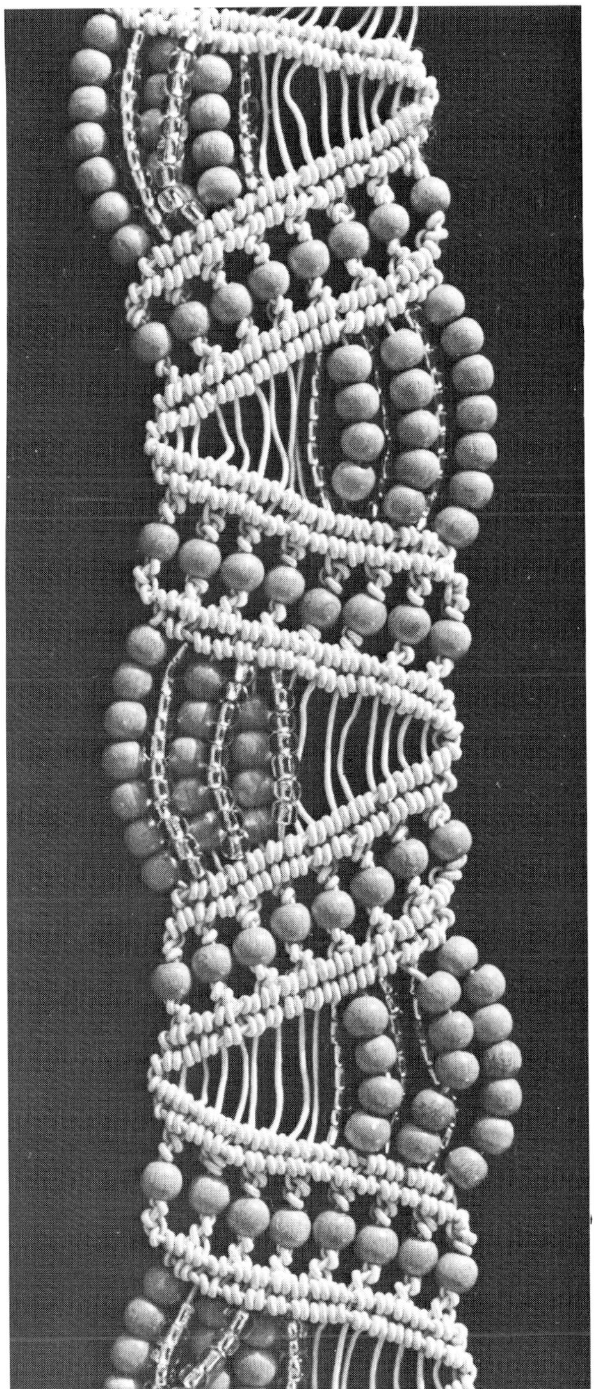

b. Piping cords, one white, one dyed navy blue, are used for this braid. Diagonal cording is worked throughout.

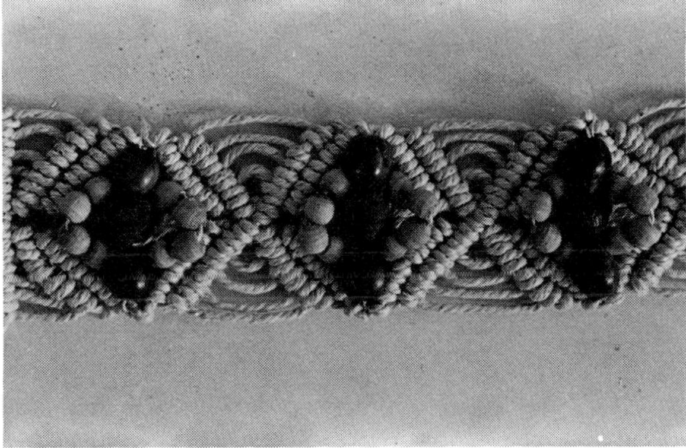

c. A traditional braid using cording in squares. Natural coloured string is used with cream and brown beads which were added after the braid was completed.

REVERSED DOUBLE HALF HITCH

The reversed double half hitch is also called a lark's head knot. It is an important knot and forms the start of many articles, being used to secure working cords on to a foundation cord, ring, or any other type of fastening. Some sources call it a cow head knot.

It can also be used to form a decorative braid. In the photograph *(left)* two sides are shown, one with the two centre cords going over the foundation cord and one with the two centre cords passing under the foundation cord. It is important when securing a number of working cords to a foundation cord to make this knot in the same way for each cord.

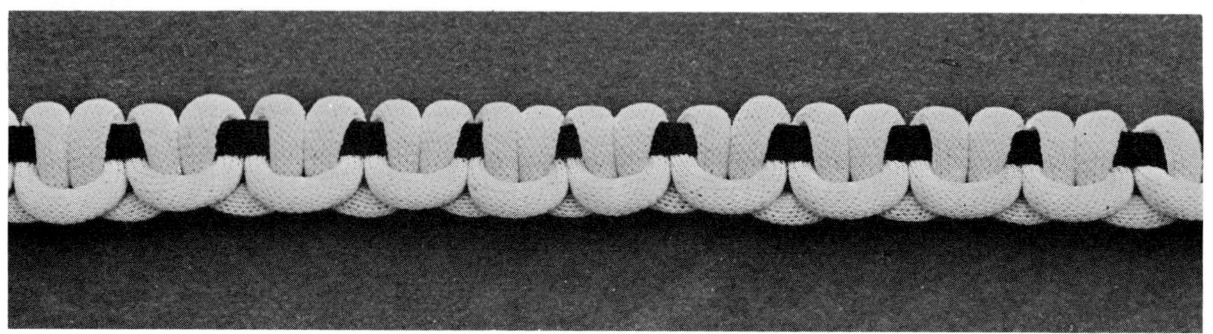

A single tatted bar, in which a half hitch is followed by a reverse half hitch.

Reversed double half hitches are used for this braid. The series is made up of two macramé runs each with a centre core. On either side of the centre core there is a red cord and a gold cord, which are used in turn to work the reversed double half hitches over the centre core. During the process of working the two runs are joined together by crossing over the gold cords from the centre. This design forms an attractive braid if made in thin soft threads, and also lends itself to a belt if thicker and firmer threads are used.

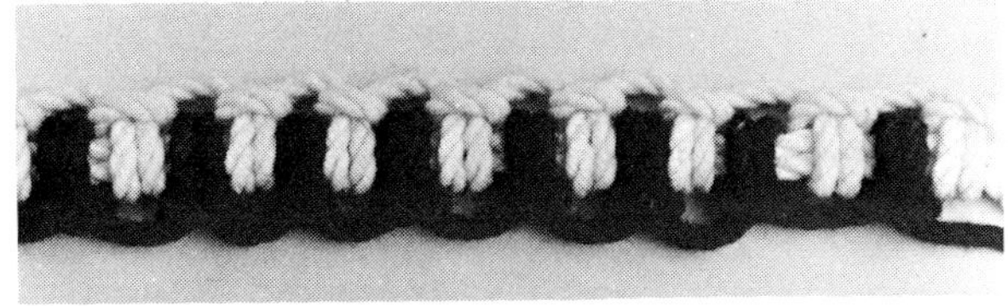

a. Double tatted bar; the reversed double half hitches are worked from alternate sides over a central core. Two colours are used for this braid.

b. A braid of reversed double half hitches in mixed gold and black cords. Two cords form the braid and no centre cord is used.

c. Groups of four half hitches form this braid. The knots are worked alternately from the right and left side. A reversed double half hitch is worked in the middle of each set of four knots. Gold lurex cords are used for this braid.

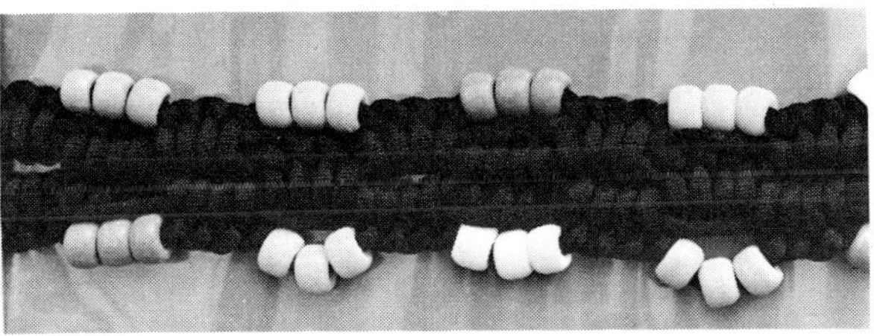

d. A braid made with half hitches in groups of four. Various china beads have been added at intervals.

e. Braid made with reversed double half hitches over a centre core, but with two working cords on each side which are used in turn, giving the looped effect on either side of the braid. Red and black tubular cords are used for this braid.

TUNIC BELT

This is a simple but most attractive belt which can be easily worked by a beginner.

It is made basically of a series of double half hitches worked vertically, but also incorporates overhand and overhand wrap knots.

The belt illustrated was made up of standard piping cord, a plain wooden ring, and a collection of various coloured wooden beads.

The belt, when laid flat, is curved to give a shaped hip fitting. The curve is formed by close knotting at the top of the belt and slightly spaced knotting at the lower edge.

The materials used for a belt to fit a 66cm waist:

5 × 730cm piping cord to form the working cords.
52 × 100cm piping cord to form the leaders.
1 × 8cm diameter wooden ring.
60 wooden beads.

The belt shown on the right is suitable for informal wear, but with a different choice of materials it would be possible to make a more sophisticated version for other occasions.

Double one of the 730cm cut lengths, from which the knots are formed, and tie a lark's head onto the wooden ring.

Repeat with the remaining four 730cm lengths of cord.

Working from the left, which is the lower edge of the belt, introduce one of the 100cm leader cords; allowing about a 30cm run-in, form the first half hitch with the working end.

Complete by working another half hitch again with the first working cord.

Repeat with the second and all subsequent eight working cords.

The first vertical line will now look like this.

On the completion of the first vertical run of cording, tie a free overhand knot at the top of the belt.

Fold the leader back and repeat with double half hitches down the belt to form the second row of

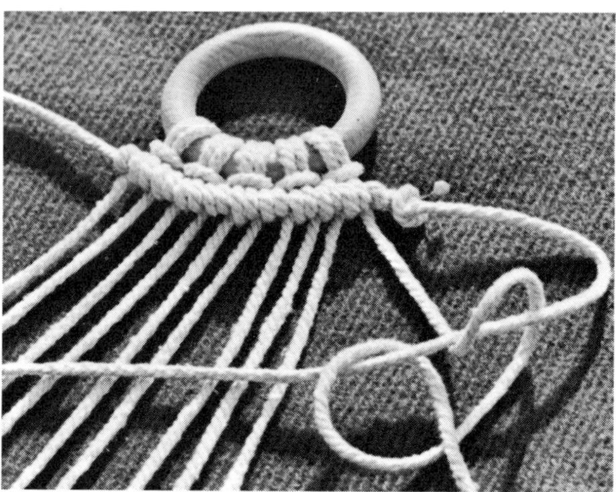

cording, leaving the remaining cord free. A pin has been used to hold the overhand knot in place.

The second row complete.

Four rows of cording have now been completed, and the loose ends of the leaders are tied together with an overhand knot.

Thread a bead on to one of the leaders and secure it with an overhand wrap knot. This is formed by winding the loose end round itself four times.

Pull the knot tight and trim.

The belt is worked to the required length and fastening is made by tying the free ends of the working cords through the ring. The ends of these cords can be decorated with beads.

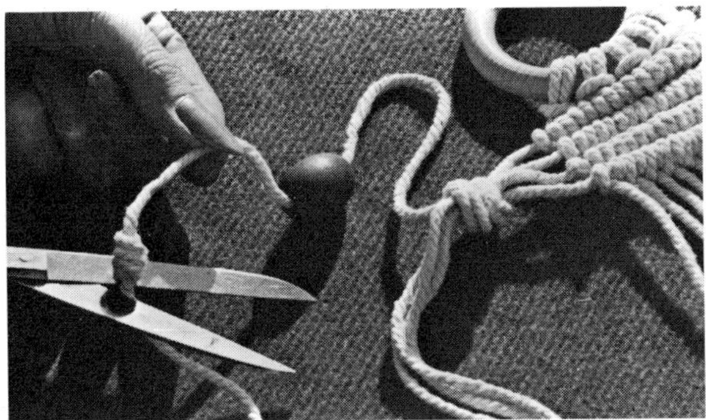

An attractive effect can be achieved by varying the levels at which the beads are knotted in place.

Here is another attractive tunic belt. It shows groups of vertical cording with decorative Josephine knots between these groups.

SLEEVE OVERLAY

A simple square knot was used to decorate the sleeve of an evening dress *(below)*. The dress shown was made in blue wool jersey fabric, the collar and lower sleeve section in cream georgette. This section was overlaid on the sleeve by working a fine piping cord which was dyed to match the blue of the dress.

It was necessary to work the macramé overlay in a continuous piece thus avoiding a seam. In the photograph below, a tin of appropriate size was covered with sheeting. A foundation thread was tied round the tin and the covering sheeting was marked at regular intervals, as shown, so that an even pattern was achieved.

One row of square knots was worked around the tin and the second row was formed by taking two cords from each knot to form the knot of the second round. Four cords are used for each knot in this example.

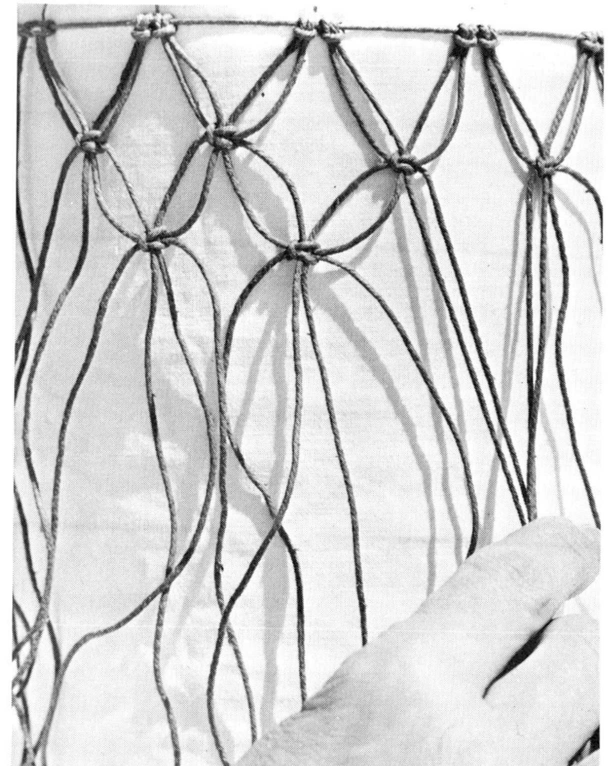

Here are some alternative forms of knotting which could have been used for the macramé sleeve overlay.

Two overhand knots joined together. One or more threads can be used for working these knots.

It is important to note the correct lay of the threads in order to achieve the attractive cluster effect.

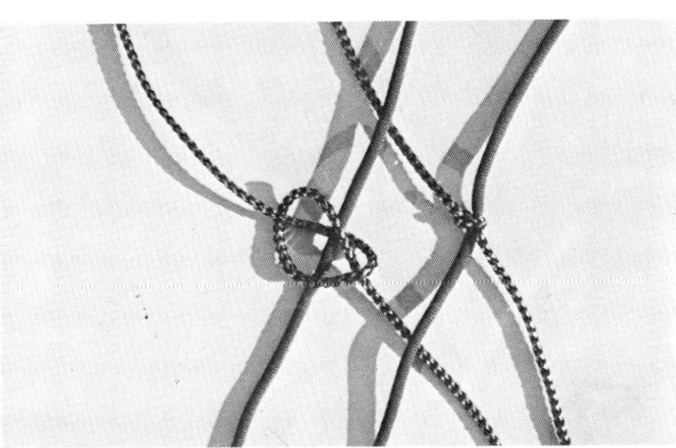

A simple overhand knot tied in one thread only over another. One or more threads, in place of the single thread shown in the photograph, may be used together to form this knot.

Simple reef knots: again, single or double threads can be used.

The reverse side of a double half hitch makes an attractive overlay. Single cords are used in the photograph. The cord on the left shows this knot being worked in a tubular rayon material.

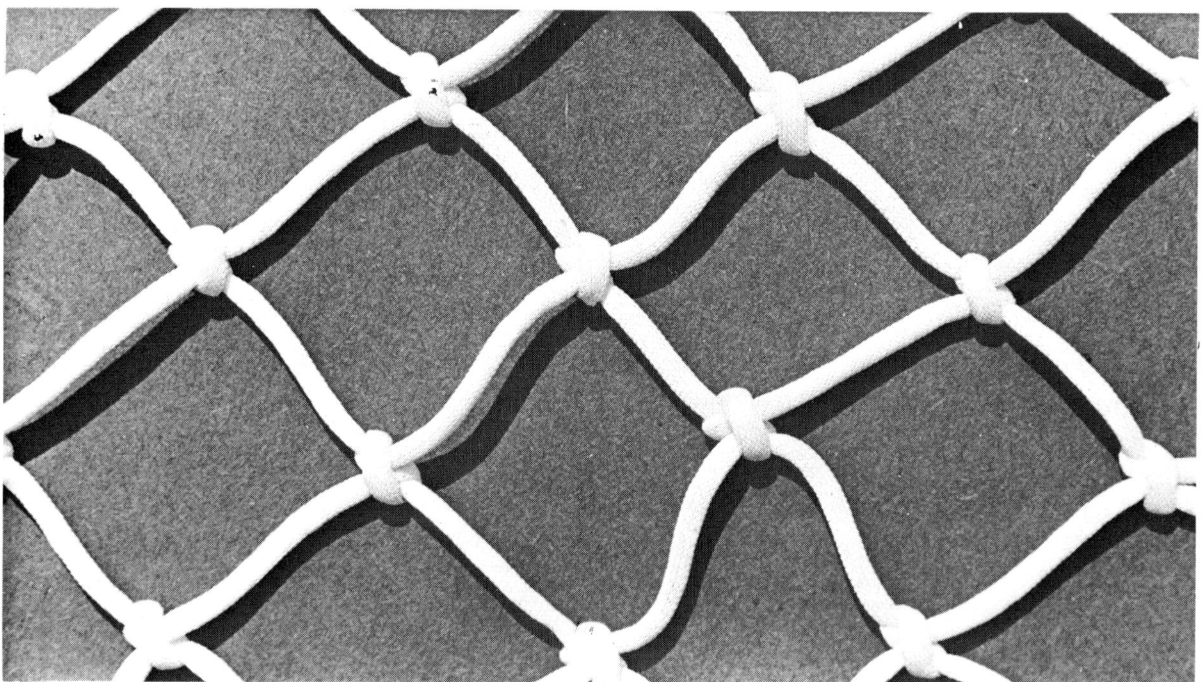

A fabric of double half hitches to show the overall effect.

In these examples the knots should be worked in rows. Each knot of the next row divides the cords from the knot of the previous row, to form the knot of the new row. The cords may be used in groups or individually. In the illustration, single cords have been used to simplify the knots; but groups of many cords, especially when working with fine cord, can be used.

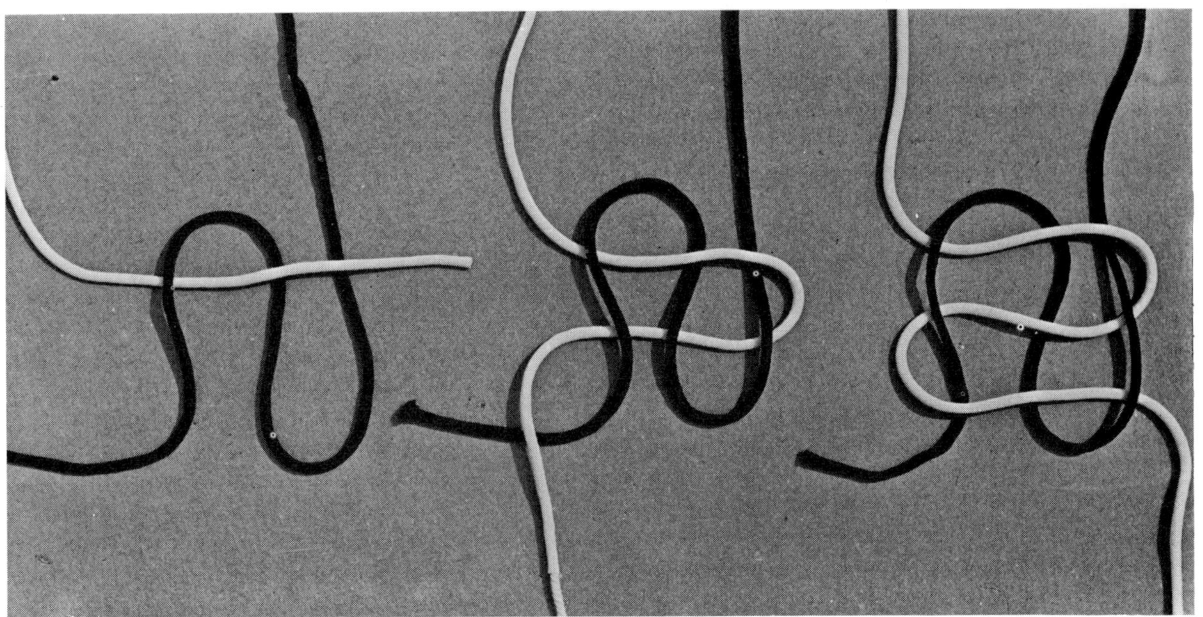

A more advanced knot, the Chinese crown *(Above)*, is particularly suitable for thicker cords and fancy threads. It could also be used for an open pattern overlay.

For simplicity in the photograph one thick cord has been used. Two or more cords could have been incorporated together, of course. The completed knot is illustrated below.

When making the sleeve covering, or indeed an overlay for any part of a garment, it is important that the overlay should equate to the shape and size of that part. In the example of the sleeve shown in this chapter, the end cords were secured in the cuff and mid-arm seams.

BELTS

The versatility of macramé is nowhere better demonstrated than in the making of belts. Belts fall broadly into two classes. The first contains multi-purpose belts which can be used on many garments, the second contains belts which are made to be an integral part of a garment's design.

No step by step instructions are given in this chapter but the examples shown can be made from the basic knots already described. The experienced worker will be able to reproduce the designs exactly but the beginner should find no difficulty in modifying them to suit his or her standard of work. Indeed, it is the primary aim of this section to inspire the reader to produce original work.

This belt is made in three different cords: gold, black, and gold and black flecked. Handmade gold beads, cording, square knots and the reversed double half hitch can be seen in this design.

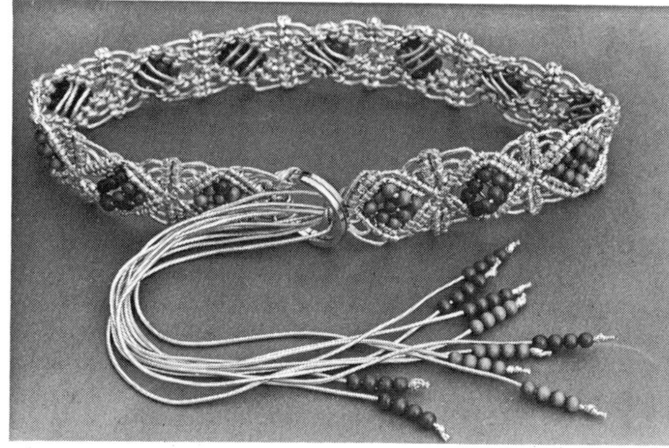

This belt is made in silver cord with pink and purple beads. Cording is used throughout. The belt is to be worn with a purple dress.

Straight choker with curtain rings

More elaborate choker

Evening cape with decorative knotted rouleau

Chunky belt in contrasting colours

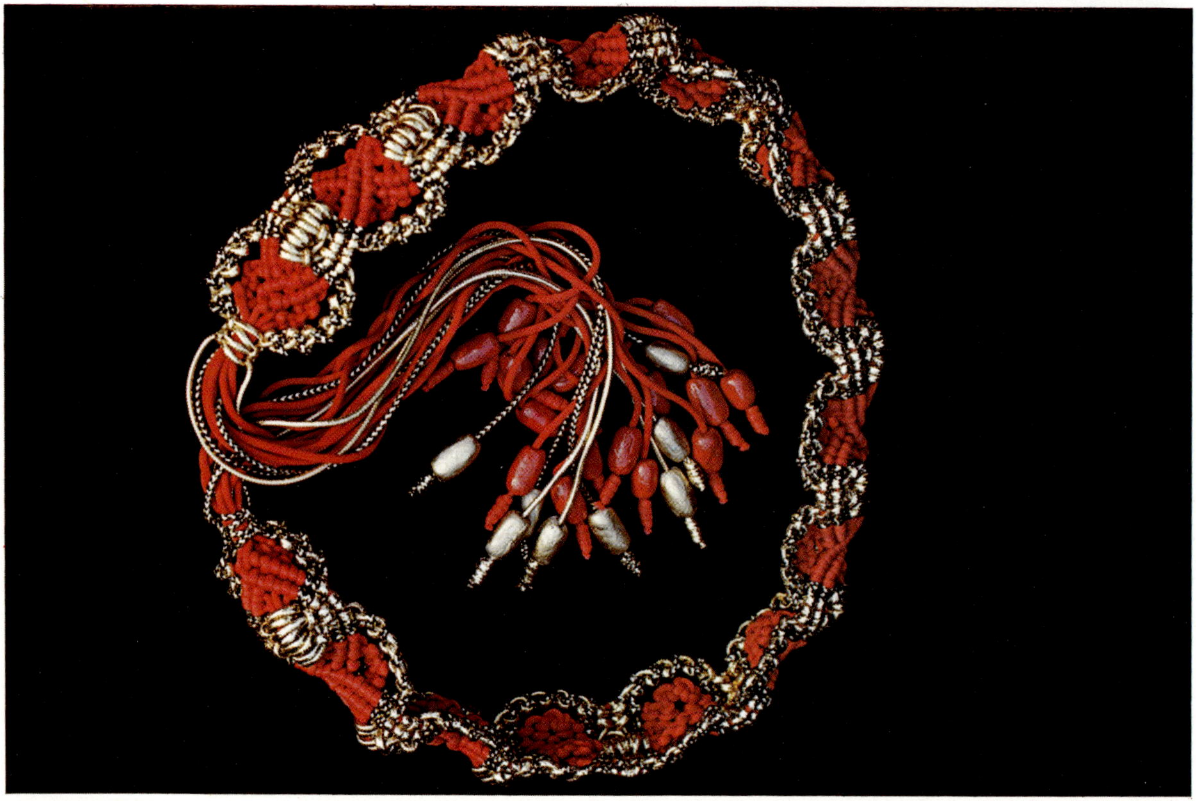

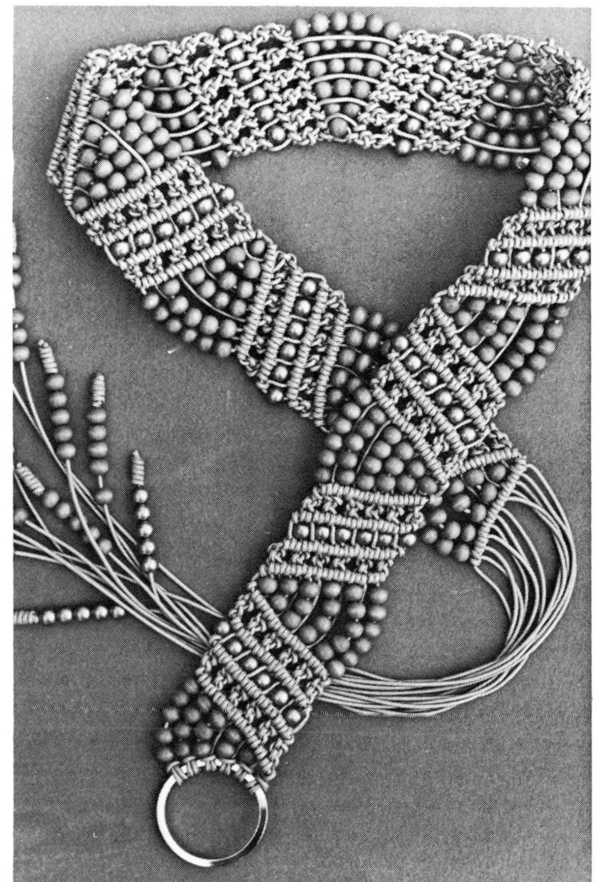

a. An interesting design of beads, cording and see-saw knots worked on a thick gold gimp. The beads are jade green and blue; a brass ring with long cords is used for the fastening.

b. Part of a belt made in soft cotton yarn with large clusters of pearls; cording, tufted square knots and half hitches are used in this design.

c. Cording forms the major part of this belt worked in a black and gold flecked cord. Shiny square black beads are used to emphasise the square in the design; a centre knot of six square knots, rolled back on themselves to form a raised ball effect, adds interest to the belt. A tie fastening is used at the back.

Belts made in traditional types of string: these belts were the first articles made by students learning to knot.

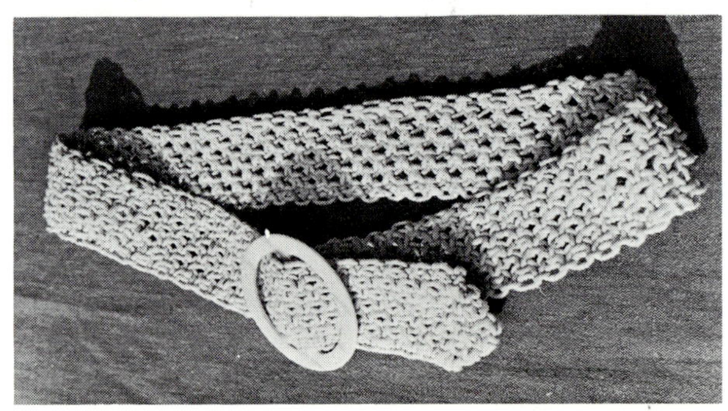

The designs below are based on the cording running through the work with see-saw knots on either side. Various materials can be used, but tubular rayon cord is used in these examples. The blackberry knot, the Chinese crown knot, the square knot and a criss-cross shape in cording are illustrated in the centres of the designs.

The chunky belt below is made in the same design as the delicate white wedding choker illustrated in the next chapter.

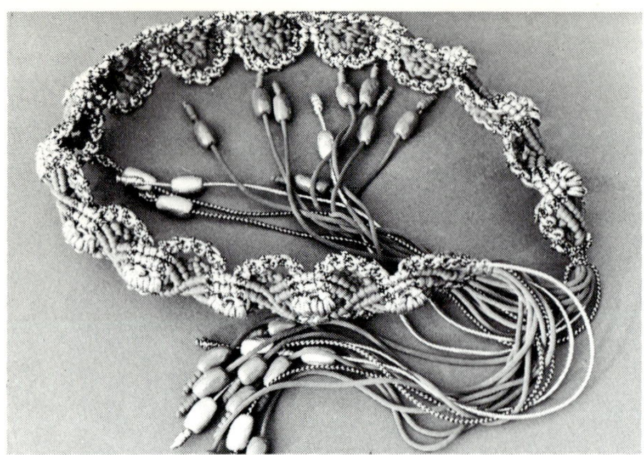

A striking belt made in gold, red, and gold flecked cord. Cording and see-saw knots form the basis of the belt, and the centre of the oval shape has a raised reversed double half hitch. The tie cords are trimmed with red and gold clay beads.

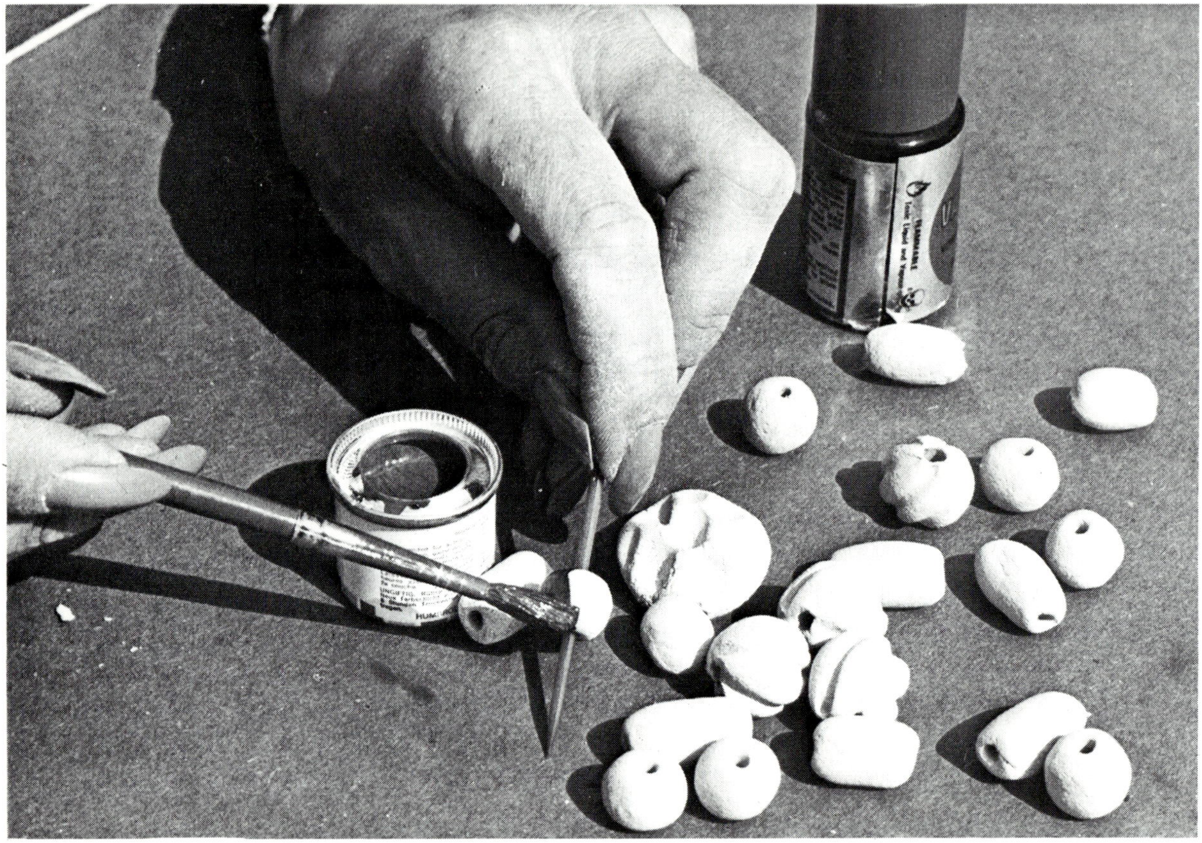

The clay beads are moulded from a proprietary brand of prepacked clay. They are easy to mould round a knitting needle to form the inner hole, and dry without firing. Various shapes and sizes can be made and, when thoroughly dry, painted to the desired colour. This is an advantage over commercial beads as the exact colour and size can be determined. Finally, the beads can be varnished to give a high gloss.

The photographs on this page illustrate further knot combinations which can be used for belts.

A firm belt made in string. Cording forms the major part of this design with the reverse side of the double half hitch knot forming the dark centre. Square knots and reversed half hitches are also used. This design lends itself to the use of two colours.

A fairly typical use of cording with square knots in the centre. This design lends itself to the use of two colours which gives an interesting effect.

Cording has been used again here to give a star shape. Beads have been added afterwards to emphasize this design. See-saw knots join the star shape.

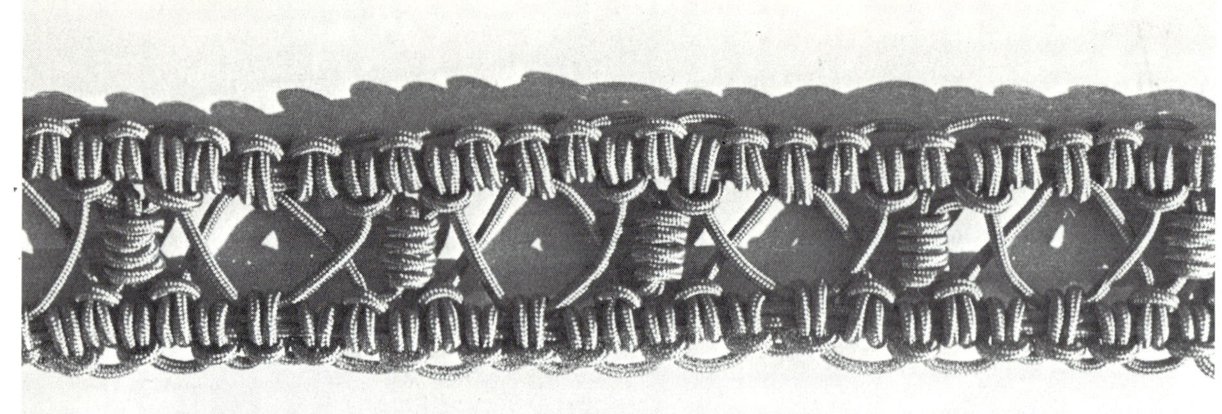

Eight cords have been used for this belt made in heavy gimp. The reversed half hitch is used throughout with an unusual coil knot used in the centre. The diagram below illustrates the method of work for this knot.

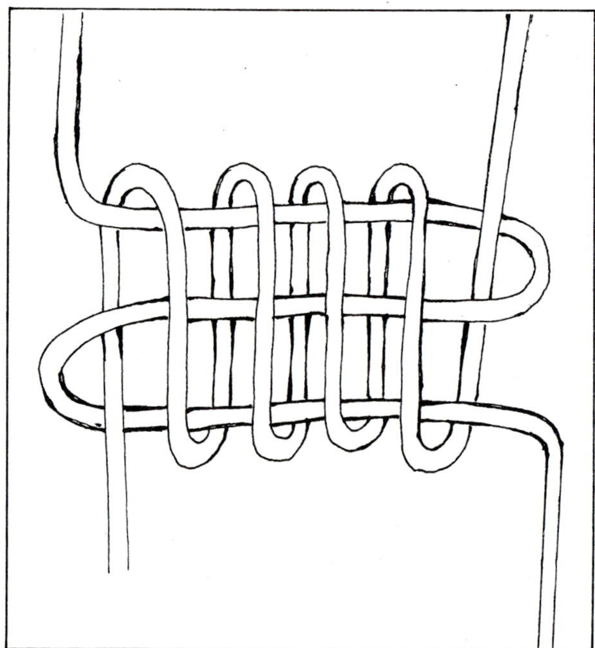

BLACKBERRY CHOKER

Giving wide opportunity for imagination and design flair, the choker lends itself particularly well to macramé work. This chapter details the stage by stage development of a fairly elaborate design incorporating a blackberry knot.

This choker is made to a similar pattern in a variety of heavyweight cords and is shown to demonstrate the importance of selecting the appropriate materials for the effect required. The choker has a variation of the reversed double half hitch worked in the centre which gives a raised effect.

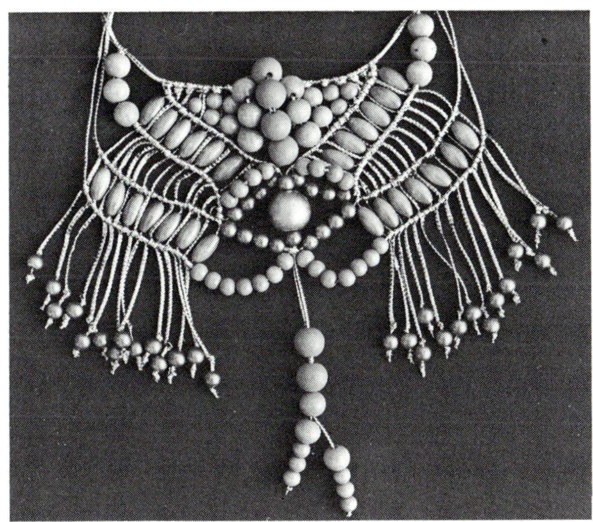

In contrast, a more dramatic choker made entirely of gold lurex cord and orange and gold beads.

The choker of this design is a wedding dress accessory made of white glacé cotton which gives a delicate effect.

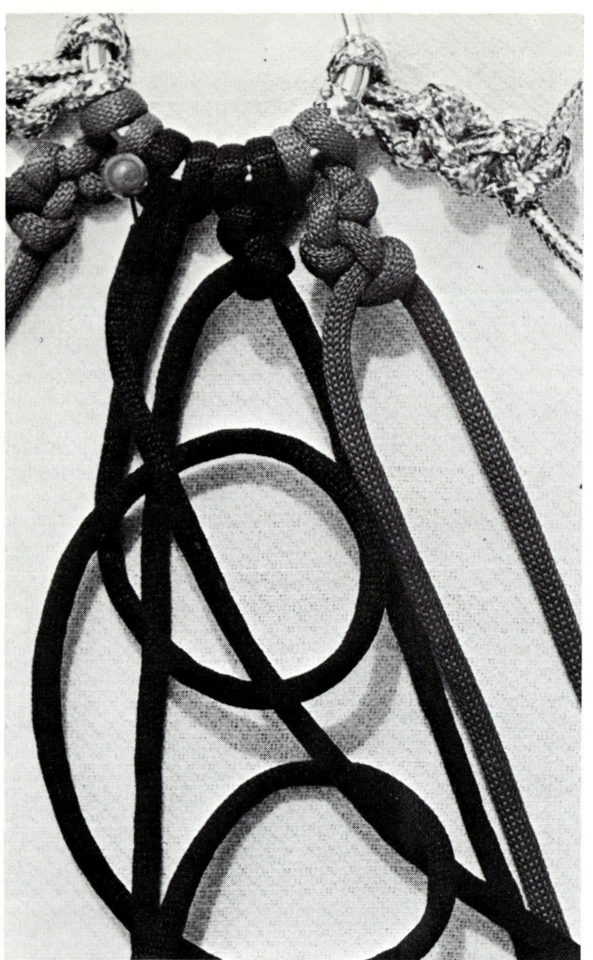

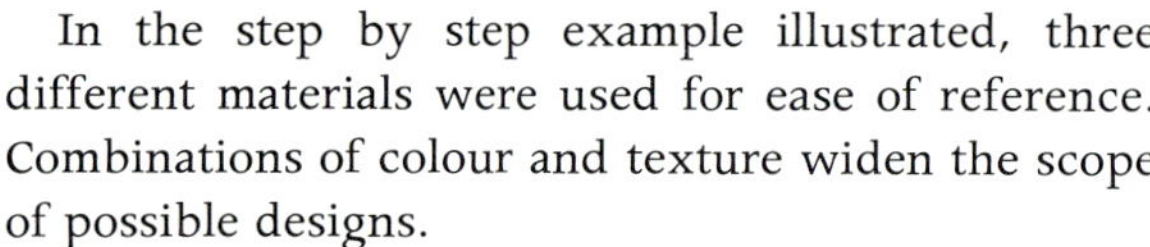

In the step by step example illustrated, three different materials were used for ease of reference. Combinations of colour and texture widen the scope of possible designs.

The first stage shows the attachment of six cords to a brass ring. The diameter of the ring depends on the dimension of the cording, but about 3cm is a useful size. A padded board was used and the ring was firmly secured to it with pins. This is important so that the working cords can be pulled tightly.

Next, tie seven half hitches alternately on the two outer pairs of cords. Tie the same knot three times on the next two pairs of cords. Take the right hand pair of centre cords and tie one double half hitch to the right, taking the left hand cord of the pair as the leader. The knot is being worked on the left hand pair of centre cords.

Using the same leader from each pair of black cords, work double half hitches to the right, tying the medium and light coloured cords. The cording to the left is started using the left black cord as the leader and working double half hitches with the medium and light coloured cords.

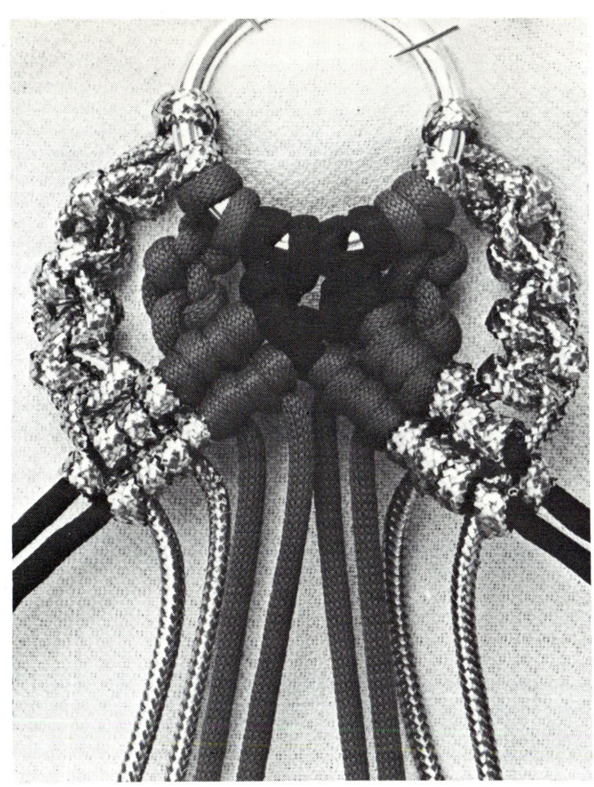

The second row of cording to the left has now been completed.

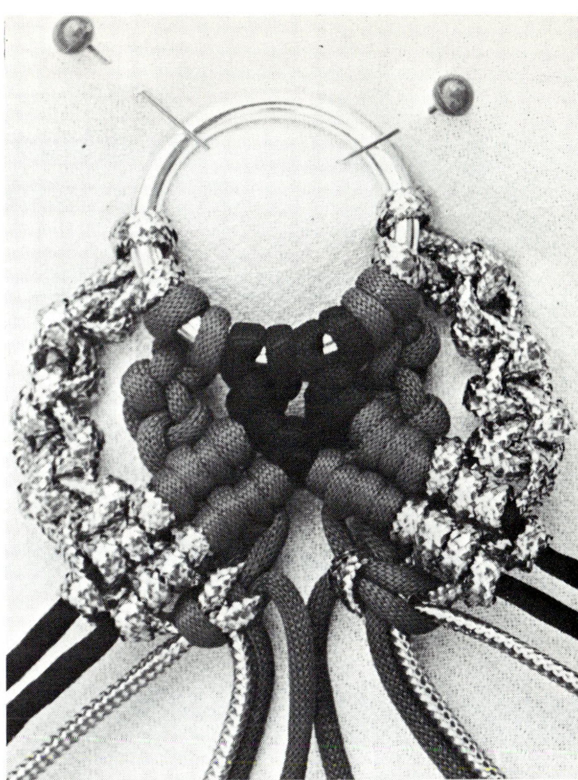

Using only the light and medium cords, tie one square knot on each side below the two cording runs.

Using the four left hand light and medium cords as leaders, take the cord nearest the centre first and work double half hitches with the right hand light and medium cords in sequence.

One row of cording to the right has now been completed.

The four rows of cording have now been completed.

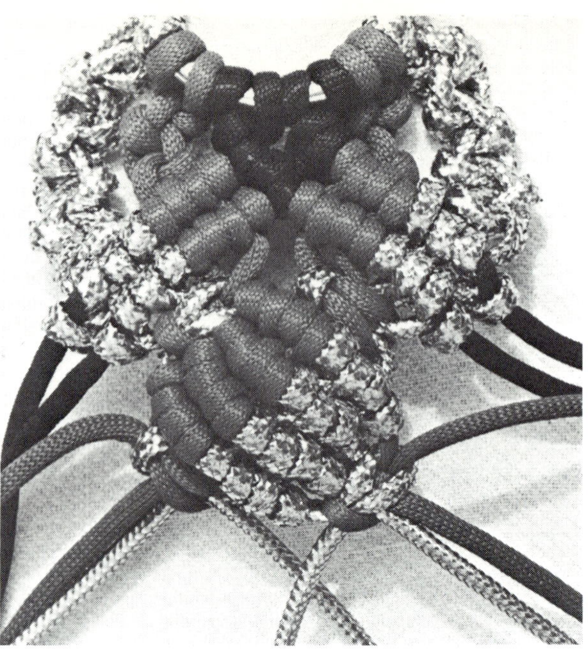

One square knot is worked on each side of the cording block.

Reintroduce the black cords as leaders; using the inner right hand cord first, work double half hitches with the four light and medium cords in sequence.

Repeat with the outer right hand black cord.

Repeat working double half hitches with the four left hand light and medium cords over the left hand black cords.

Using the four centre black cords, work two sets of double half hitches.

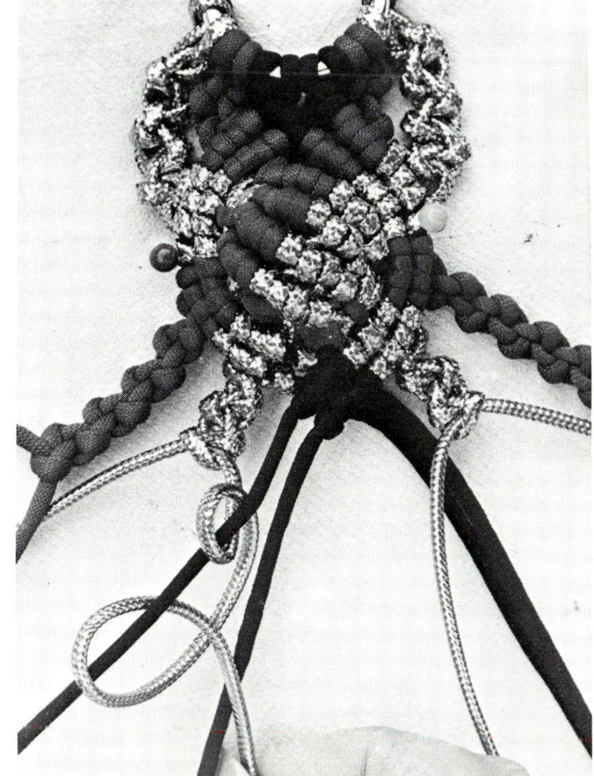

Work alternate half hitches on the light and medium cords—nine on the medium colour and five on the light.

The second pattern has now been started by working double rows of cording to the left. Take the black cords as leaders and work to the left and then to the right, working double half hitches with the light and medium coloured cords.

Care should be taken, when working the cross-over of the cording between the blackberry knot, to place the double rows of cording in the right direction, ie right over left or left over right. This depends on which line of cording is worked first.

BEADED NECKTIE

The making of a tie like the one illustrated lends itself to the free use of beads and knotting runs.

The tie shown on the right is an example of what can be achieved, but is not exactly the same as the one demonstrated in the following instructions. Red string was used in conjunction with various shades and sizes of red and orange beads. The step by step photographs show the development of a complicated design but it can be easily modified to produce a simpler tie.

The foundation band is formed from a series of square knots worked on four cords. The threads are attached to one side of the fastener. The square knots were worked to the position of the 'front fall'. The working cords of the fall are attached by lark's head knots over three cords only. The remainder of the band was completed and tied to the other part of the fastener.

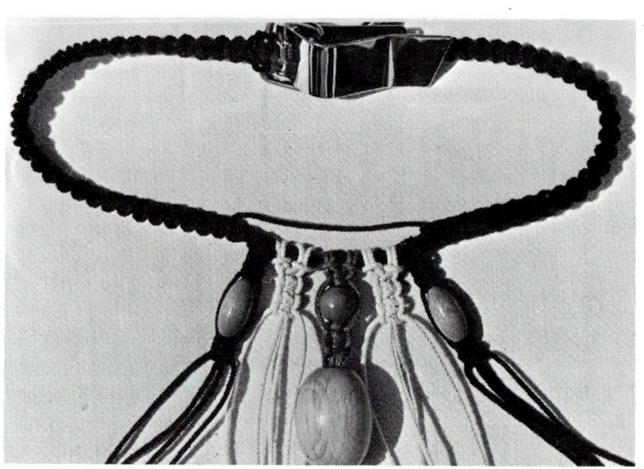

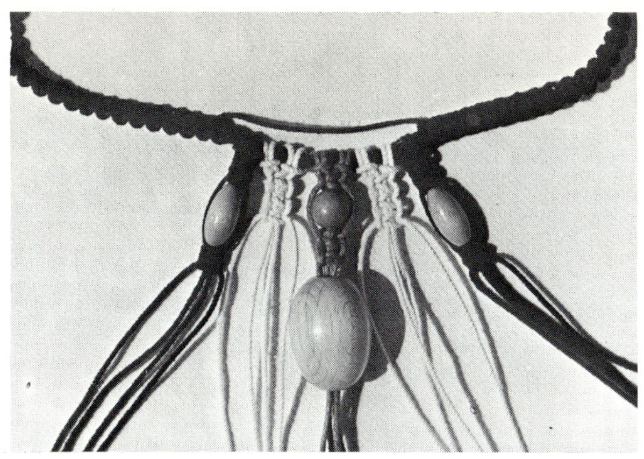

The fall is made up of ten lengths of cord looped over the cords of the band, thus producing twenty working lengths.

On each set of four cords, square knots were worked and beads threaded on to the two centre cords at intervals. The two outside cords lock each bead in place with a square knot.

The larger bead in the centre was threaded with the four cords.

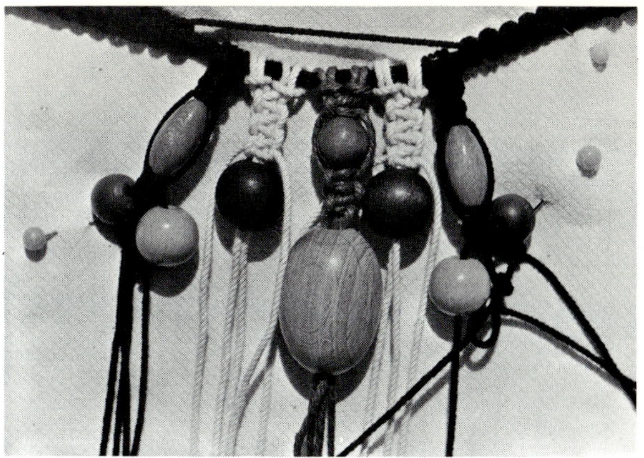

Beads were added to the two outside cords of the set of four dark cords. Using the outside cords as leaders, horizontal cording was then worked to hold the beads in place.

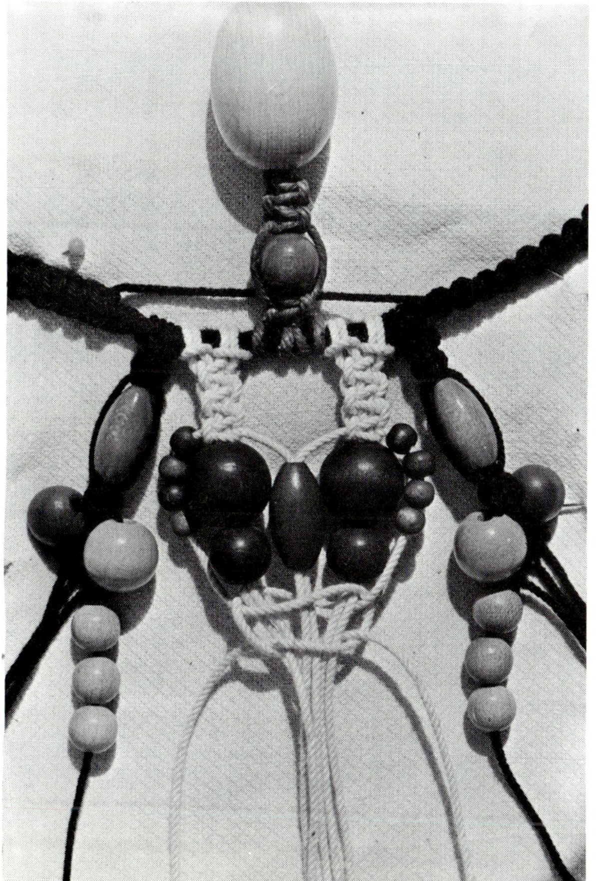

To show the underneath working, the large centre bead and cords have been lifted and a bead pattern has been built up on the light cords. A square knot holds these in place. Additional small beads have been placed on the black cord leader.

The large bead and centre cords have now been replaced. The bead is held in place by the black cord leader and the beginning of a three dimensional form is produced.

Using the outside black cord as the next leader, work double half hitches with the light threads to form a cording pattern.

This cording has now been completed.

The leader of each row of cording from both sides is tied into a square knot over all the centre cords. This is repeated with each leader.

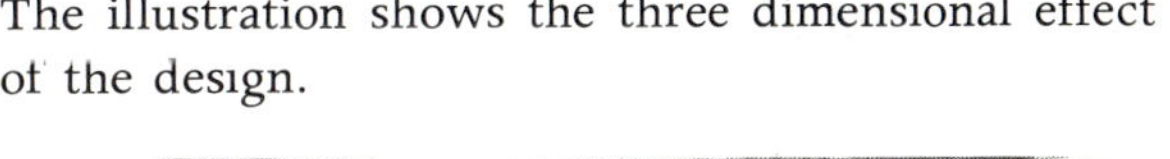

The illustration shows the three dimensional effect of the design.

The knotting for the tie has been completed and the free cords can now be used for development and embellishment.

BEADED COLLAR

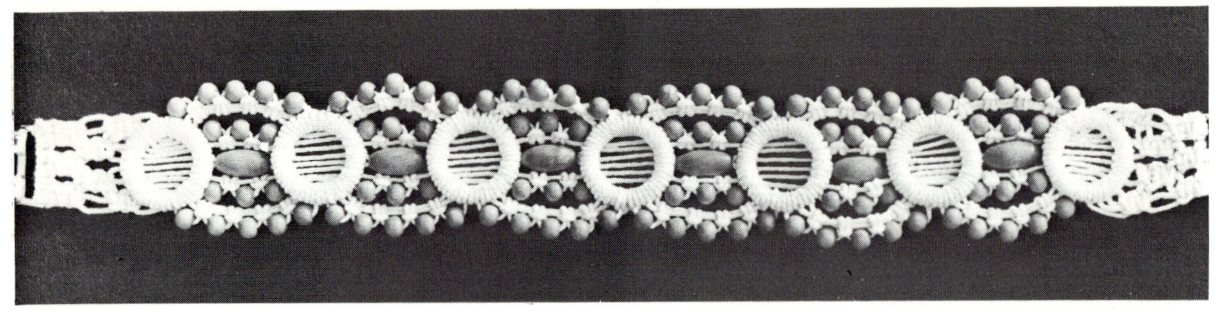

This is an example of a straight beaded collar using white glacé cord, coloured wooden beads, and 3cm diameter white plastic rings.

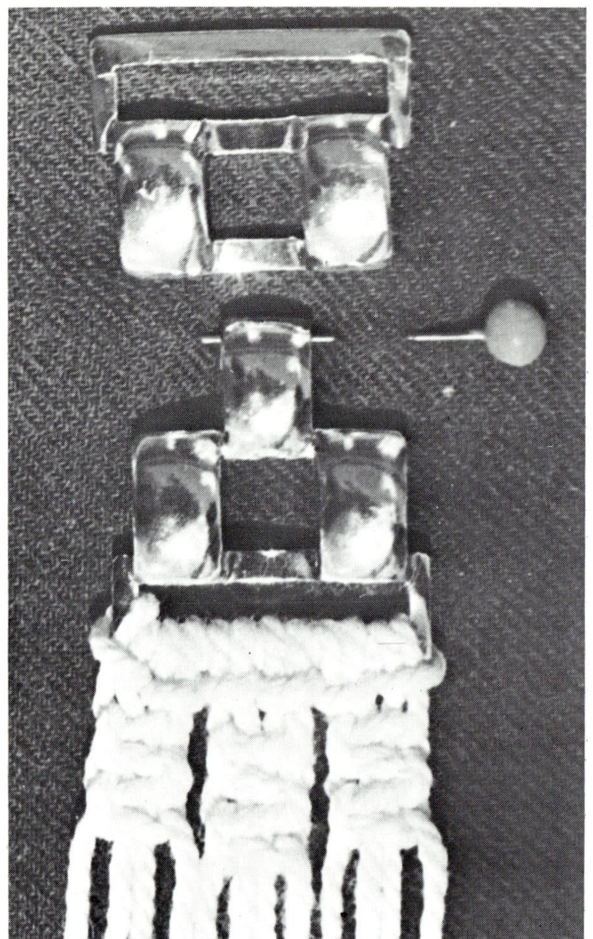

Six cords are secured to a silver plated square fastening with a lark's head knot. The fastening is securely anchored with a pin to a work board. Two square knots are worked on each set of four cords.

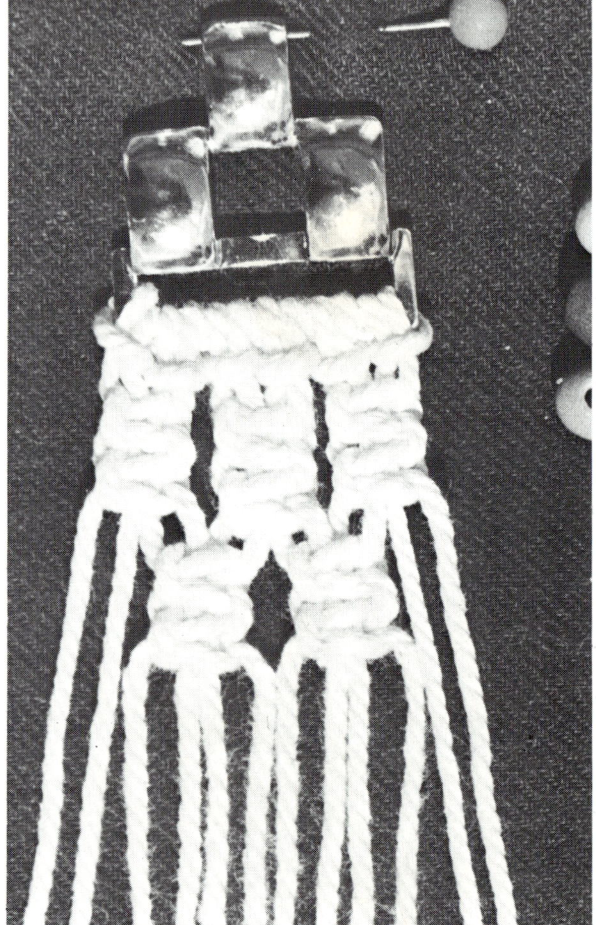

Using the eight inner cords, tie two square knots on each set of four cords.

Belt of beads, cording and see-saw knots

Silver ear-rings

A pair of evening sandals

Flowing evening dress gathered in with macramé belt

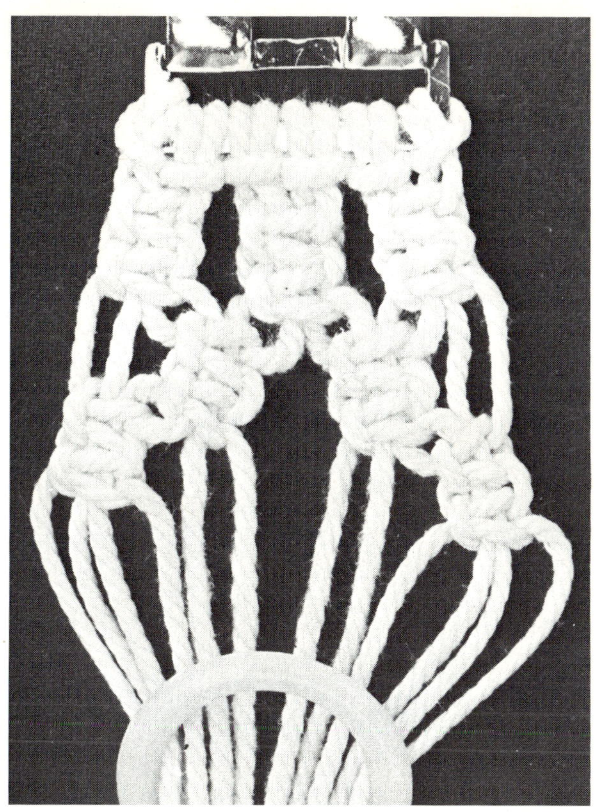

Two square knots are worked using the four outside cords. All the cords are then inserted through the plastic ring.

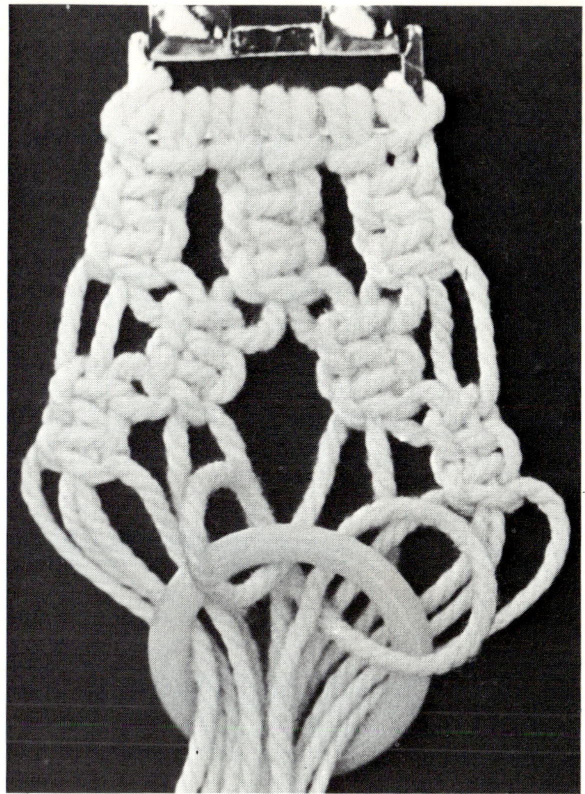

Using the ring as the leader, work double half hitches with each cord in turn, starting from the centre.

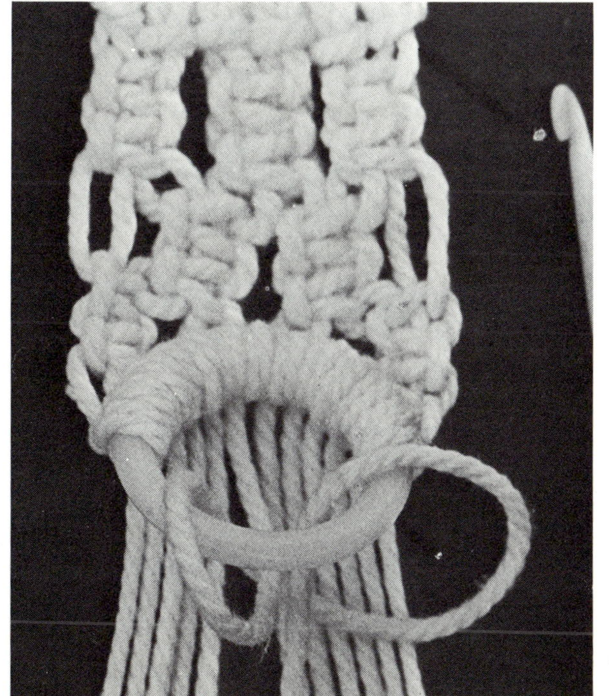

All the cords have now been tied covering half the ring.

Again taking the centre cords first, repeat the process, which will result in the complete covering of the ring; a crochet hook is a useful aid in completing this stage.

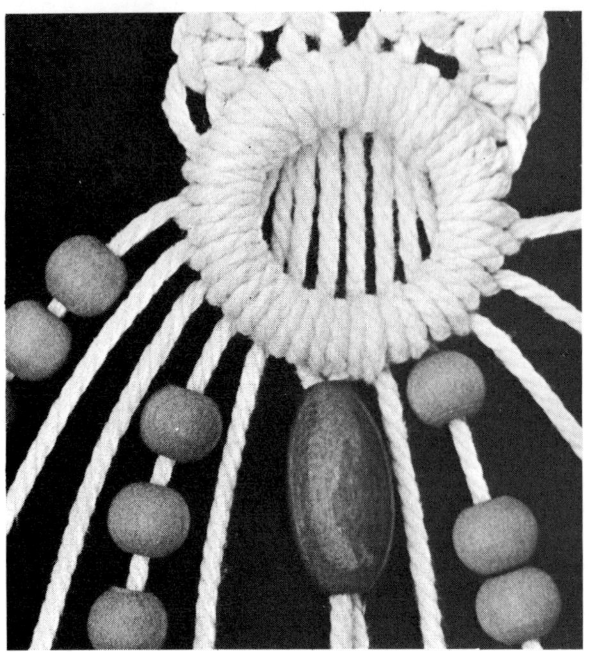

The ring has now been completely covered and the beads have been threaded on the cords. Thread five beads on the outer cords, then miss two cords, place three beads on the next cord, and one large bead on the two centre cords.

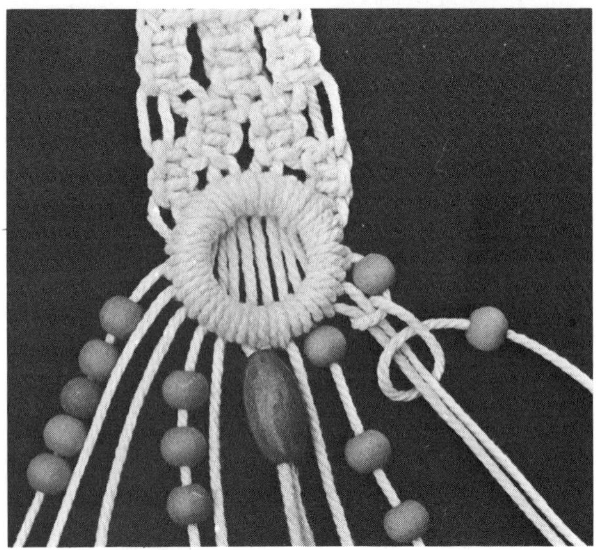

All the beads are in place and the first bead of the outer row is being locked in place with a reversed half hitch (lark's head knot).

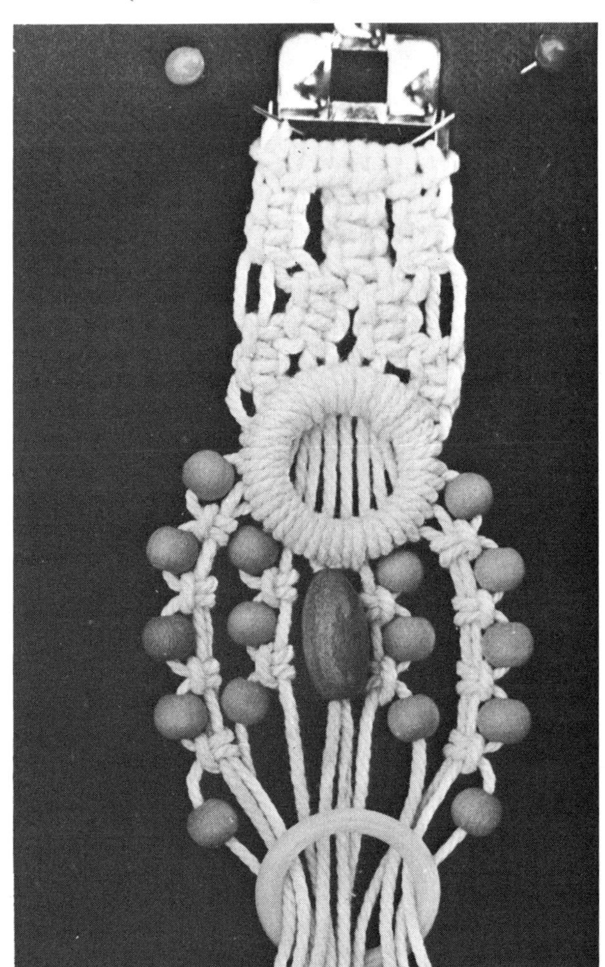

The remaining beads have now been tied into place and the second ring has been introduced. Seven rings were used in this collar.

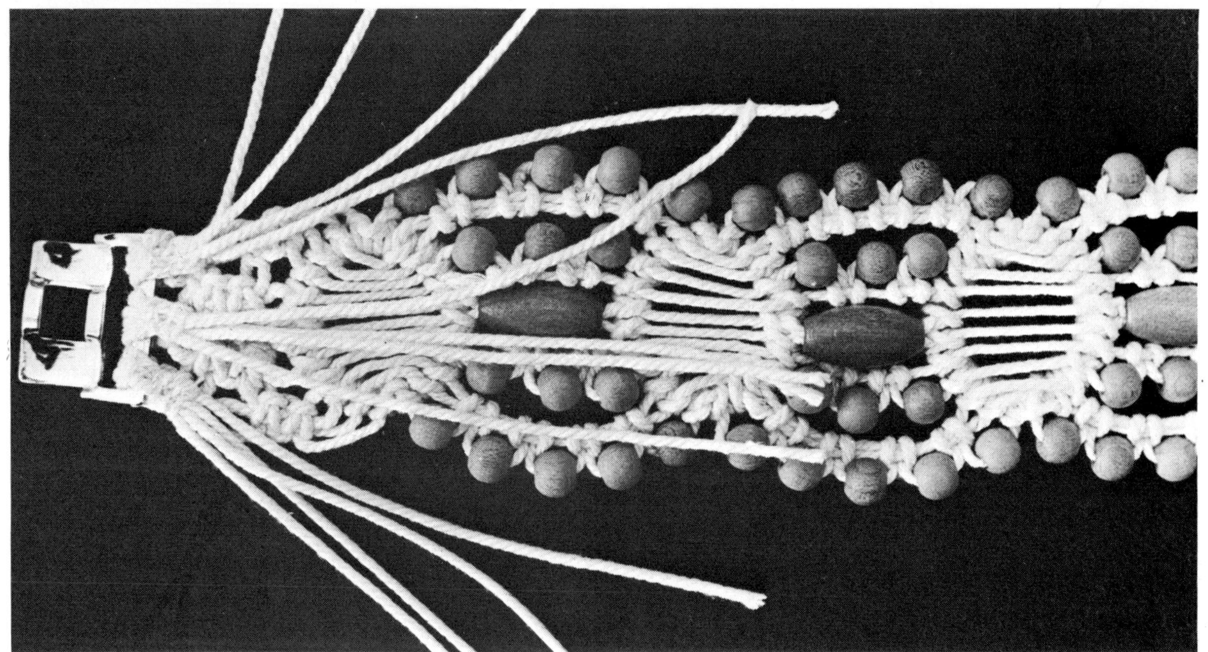

When the collar is completed, the working ends are threaded through the female end of the fastener and the raw ends are sewn down before trimming.

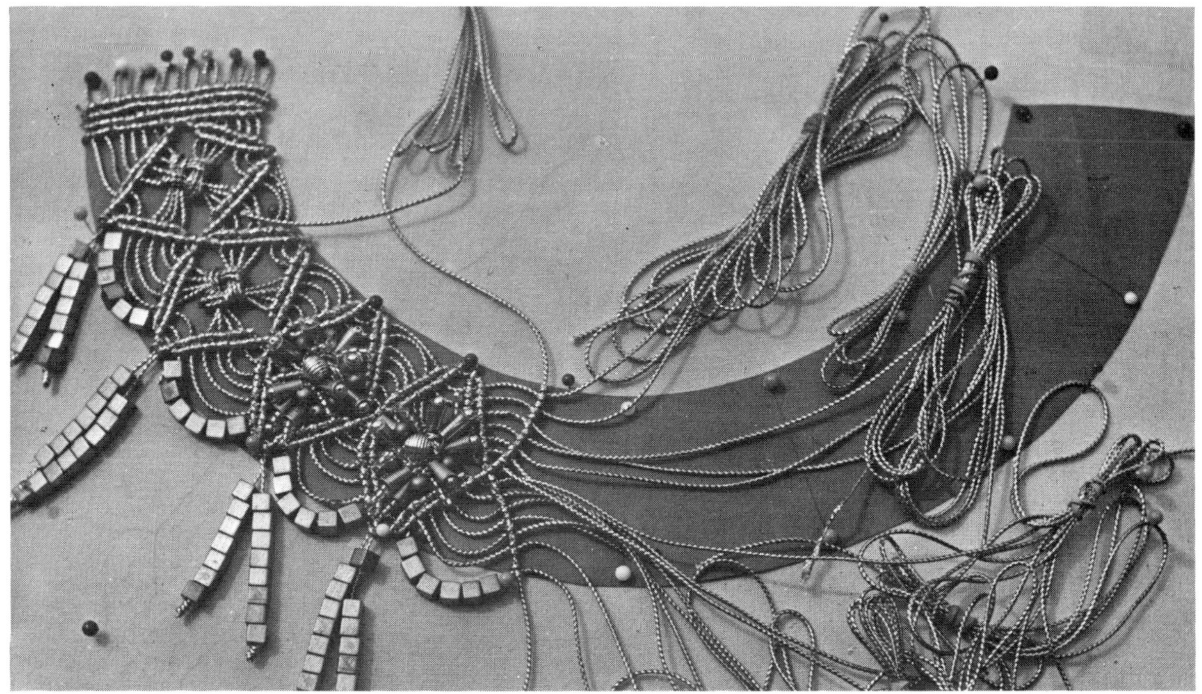

The collar described in this chapter is an unshaped one, and is therefore suitable only for a narrow design. The photograph above shows work in progress for a broader shaped collar. It is necessary to work the knotting over a paper pattern shape which has been previously pinned to the work board. The knotting is pinned at regular intervals over the pattern to follow the shape. Some of the centre knots seen in the photograph have been covered with beads.

GOLD BRAIDED FRINGE

This attractive black evening dress *(above)* was designed to incorporate pin tucking and gold macramé work.

The macramé pattern, while appearing complex, was in fact fairly simple to work.

The success of the dress depended to a great extent on the choice of contrasting fabrics. A matt black fabric was used for the pin tucking, a shiny black satin for the main part of the dress, and an unusual gold thread for the decoration. Black beads were used to complete the fringe.

The pattern is based on a traditional macramé crossover design using cording and square knots.

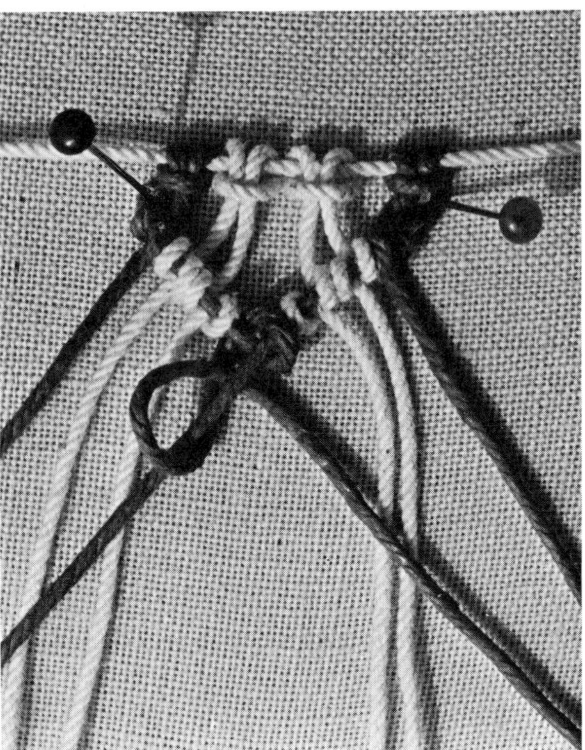

Four cords are used for the braid. The cords are anchored to a foundation cord by a lark's head knot producing eight working cords in total. Pins are used to hold the cords in place. The two outer threads are used as the leaders, while the inner six threads form the cording with double half hitches. The cross-over pattern to the left has been started. Light and dark cords have been used to clarify the details in the illustrations.

The cording to the left has been completed and the cording to the right has been started.

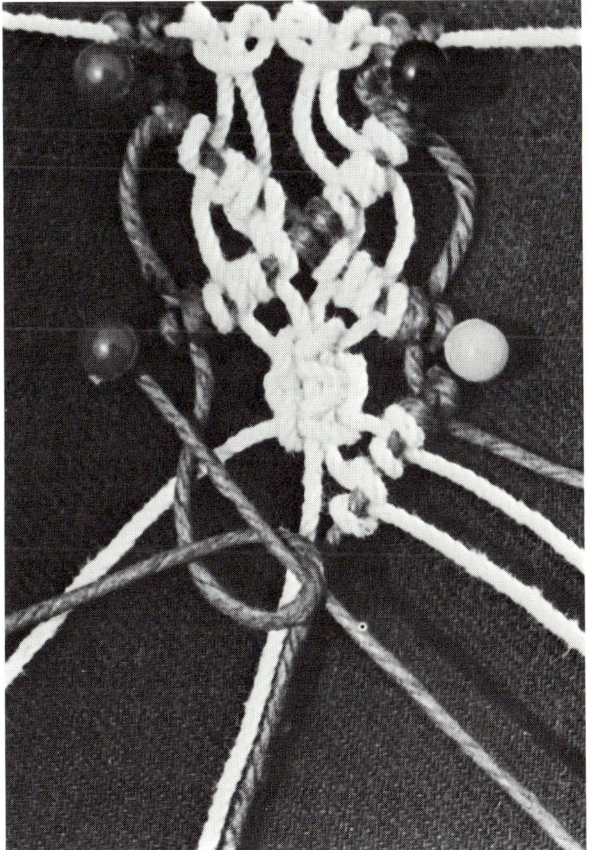

Two square knots have been formed in the centre. The repeat pattern of cording is being worked and the outer points are held firmly in place with pins. It is important to check the width of the braid at this point, in order to keep the width constant through the working of the braid.

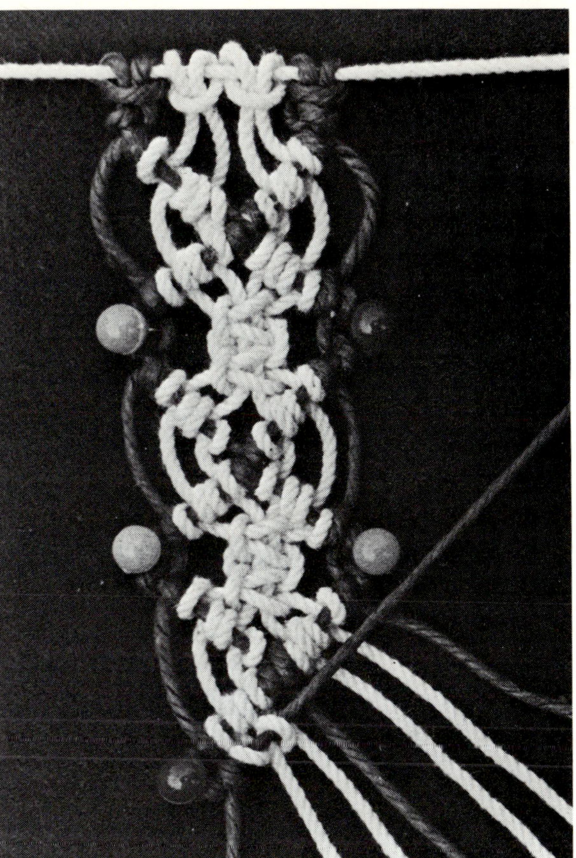

When the required length of straight braid has been worked, a corner is formed.

To work this corner, a pin is placed at the apex of the corner to hold the leader in place. The leader is held parallel to the completed row of cording and a second row is worked.

The cording from the apex is complete and the next pattern is being started. The centre dark cord is used as the leader and is worked to the left.

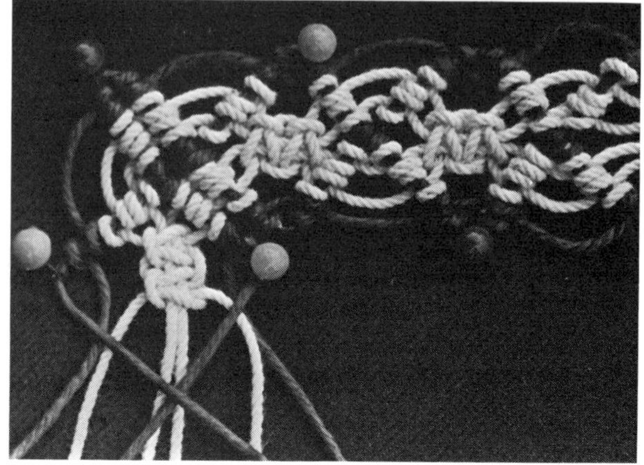

The corner is now complete and the design follows through the normal run of knotting.

A closeup of the braid to show the fringe being attached to the loose outside cords of the braid. A short length of cord is knotted with a lark's head knot, and a wooden black bead is secured by working an overhand knot on either side of the bead on the cut ends.

It is not always easy to decide what direction a design will take at a corner. The use of a mirror placed across a completed straight run of work, at the correct angle, will help to establish the design of the pattern round the corner.

This completed square neckline braid illustrates the working of two corners in a different design.

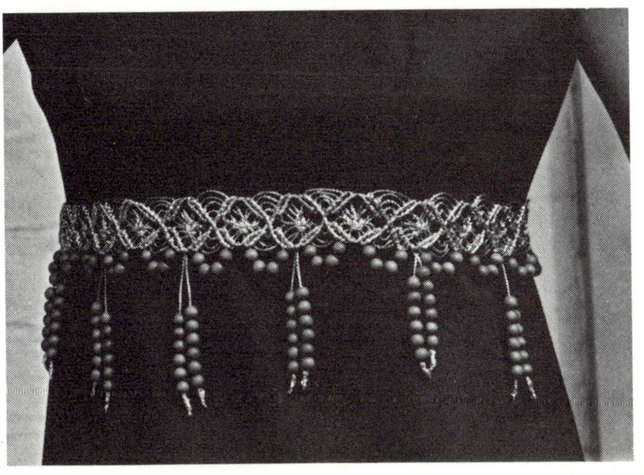

This braided dress decoration illustrates the use of beads and a beaded fringe. Silver lurex cord and a traditional regular macramé pattern were used. The braid is placed on the under bustline of an Empire style evening dress made of French navy blue crêpe fabric.

SANDAL TOPS

The tying of sandal tops demonstrates the versatile way in which macramé can be used to form shapes in different dimensions. Different threads and the application of beads have been used in the making of the designs shown here.

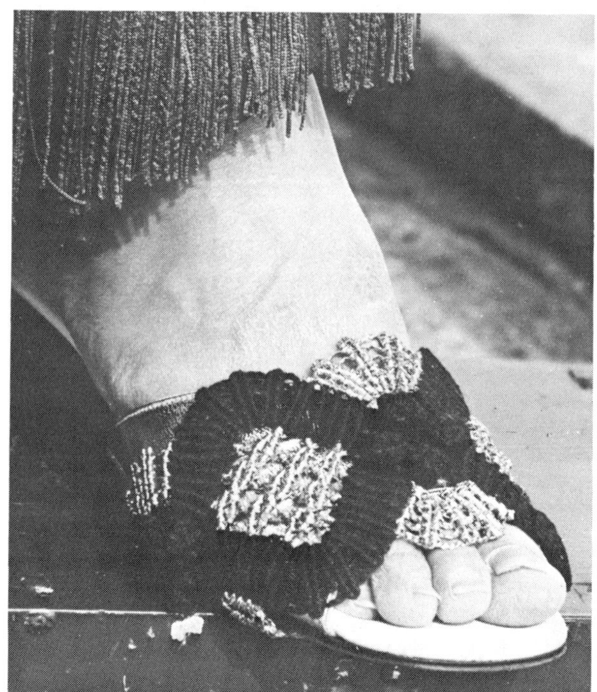

The design was sewn onto a silver leather mule and the macramé decoration was made of black and silver cords.

(Above) The sole of the sandal on the right was cut by a shoemaker from cork, and the macramé was glued with rubber based adhesive to the top of the sole which was then covered with soft leather.

These sandals were made of gold and black lurex cord formed round a brass ring. The sole was deep cork and the lining gold kid.

The method for working these sandal tops is shown in the following illustrations. A paper pattern of the sandal top should be made as a guide for the required shape. This can be done simply by folding and cutting a piece of paper over the foot. The final adjustment is made by fitting the completed work snugly over the foot before gluing the macramé to the sole. The sandal design is symmetrical and is worked from side to side, both feet being the same.

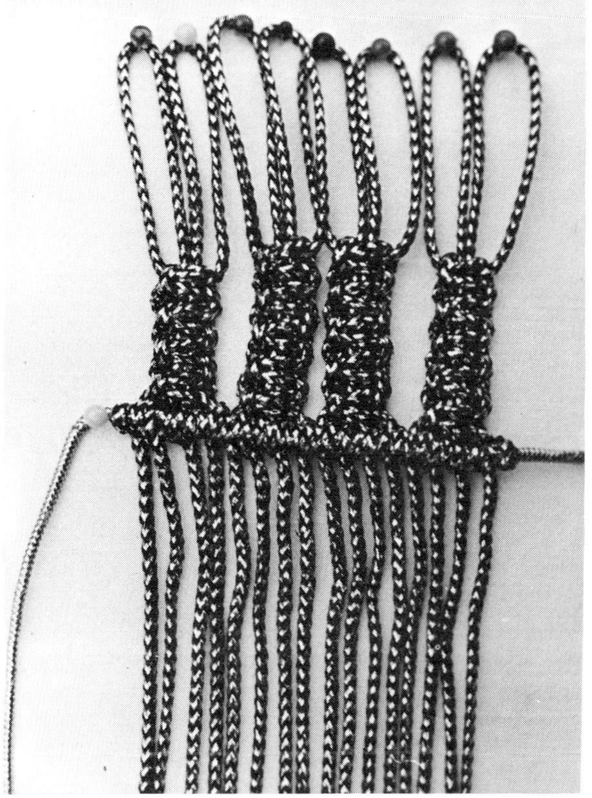

The knotting is started at the front with eight looped working cords, each cord being about 2 metres long. They are anchored to a work board. Square knots are worked before attaching the separate cross leader to form the central outer cording square. The right hand end of the cross leader forms the centre front of the sandal.

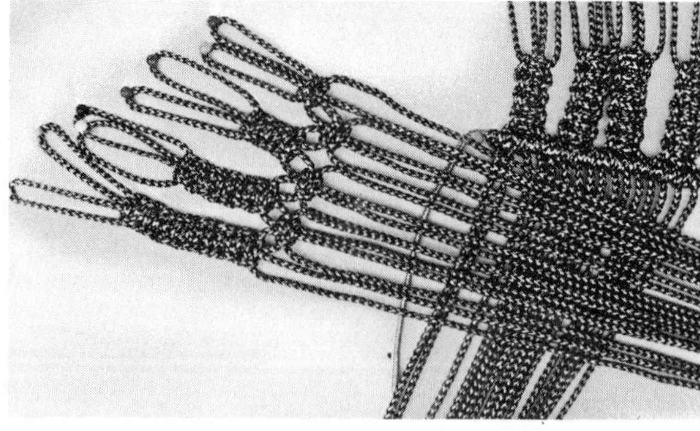

The back half of the sandal upper, again with eight looped working cords 2 metres long, has now been introduced. The number of square knots is increased towards the heel to form the foot shape. Three square knots are made to join the cords together.

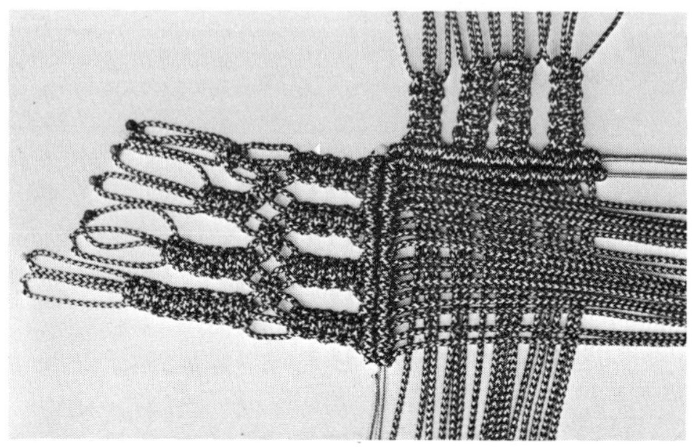

More square knots complete the side and the leader is turned down ready for cording. The cording is completed on the second side of the square and a second leader is added and corded.

The twenty-four cords are then divided into three groups, eight on the outside and sixteen in the centre. The brass ring is fastened in place with pins. The cords are now looped in the ring.

The third side of the square is being worked with two rows of cording. Ensure that the sides are of equal length.

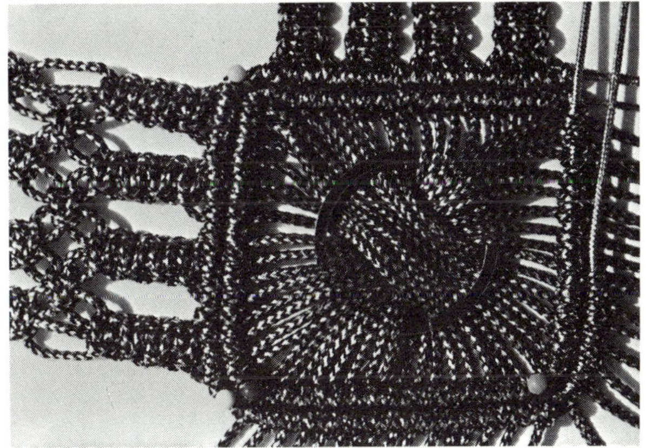

The fourth side of the square is almost completed.

The square knots are being tied to make the other side of the shoe. The design for this knotting follows the pattern of the first side.

BAGS

A macramé bag adds to the range of fashion accessories. Harmony can be achieved by emphasising the same series of knots in each accessory if a bag is to match a belt or choker already made.

Although the following examples bear no direct relationship to the belt and choker designs in previous chapters, the worker can modify the designs to produce a relationship.

The following designs suggest casual use but macramé bags are of course suitable for formal occasions. Evening bags, for example, could be made of Russia braid and lurex threads with beads.

Handles can be purchased from most haberdashery stores, or suitable shapes may be cut from plywood. These shapes can then be painted, varnished, or covered with leather or PVC. Care should be taken with the selection of handles as the choice can make or mar the overall effect.

The purpose of the bag will determine the type of lining used, if a lining is required. A waterproof plastic lining would be a useful addition to a beach bag, for instance. Linings are attached by hemming in place after the macramé work is completed.

Circles of white plastic tubing and coloured beads were used to make this shoulder bag. White piping cord is used for the knotting but any other type of string cording could be used. The overall size is 30cm and the bag is 8cm deep. The method of working the bag is shown on the following pages.

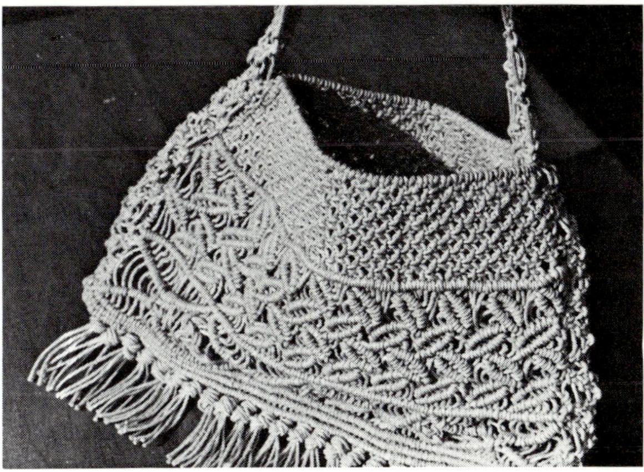

Three designs are illustrated. The bags are made in string, the traditional material for this type of design. String is hard wearing and easy to work. Attractive handles have been chosen, one bag having a string cord.

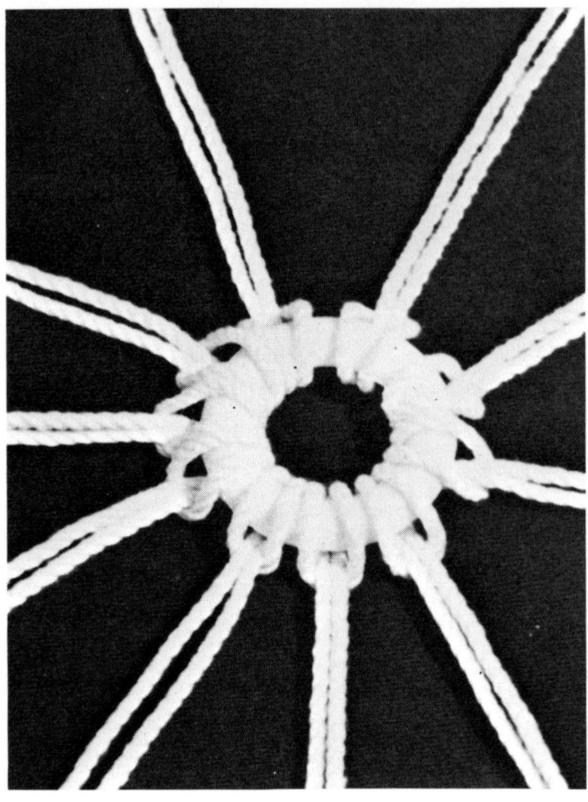

A white plastic ring 5cm in diameter forms the centre. Ten cords are anchored by a lark's head knot over the centre ring.

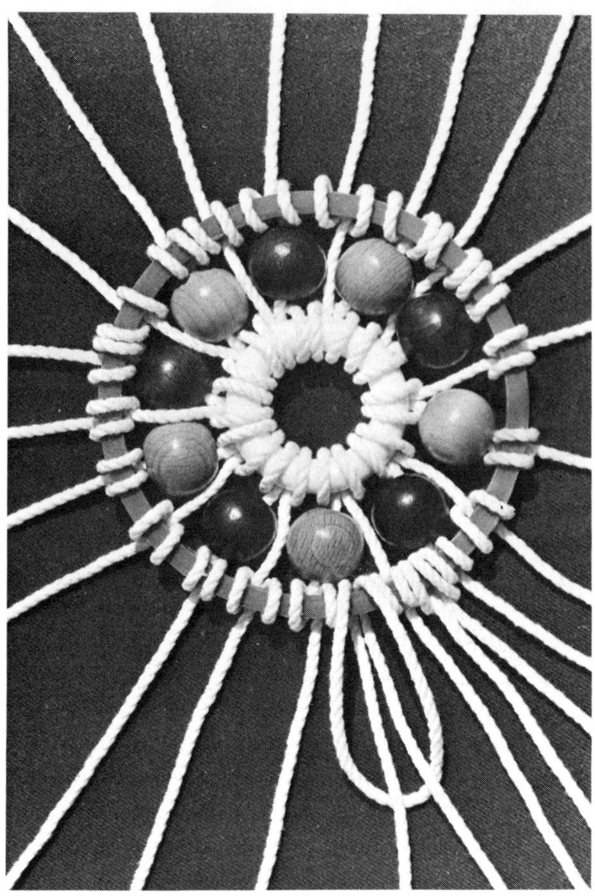

Ten coloured wooden beads are then threaded on alternate cords. A second ring of plastic tubing, 12cm in diameter, is used as the leader, the working cords being placed over it with double half hitches. Additional cords are placed between each double half hitch (twenty additional cords are added in all). In the photograph, one extra cord has been added and another is being tightened. The lark's head knot is clearly seen in the lower part of the photograph.

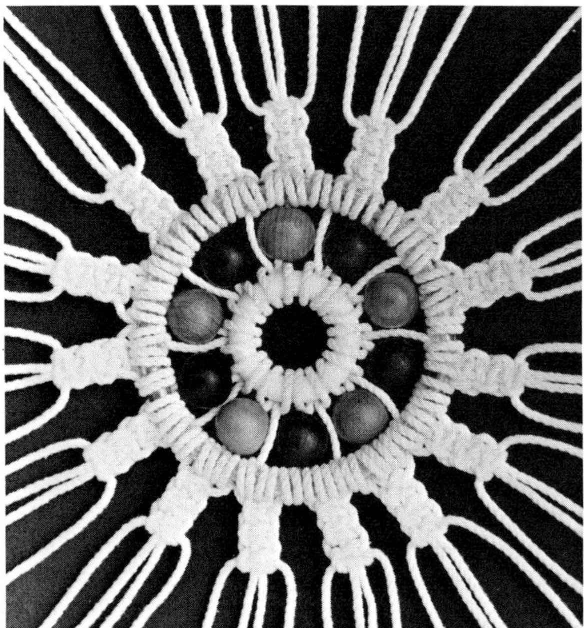

Three square knots are worked on each set of four cords.

Four square knots are then worked on four cords dividing the cords from the knot above. A third plastic ring, 27cm in diameter, is added and double half hitches worked over it.

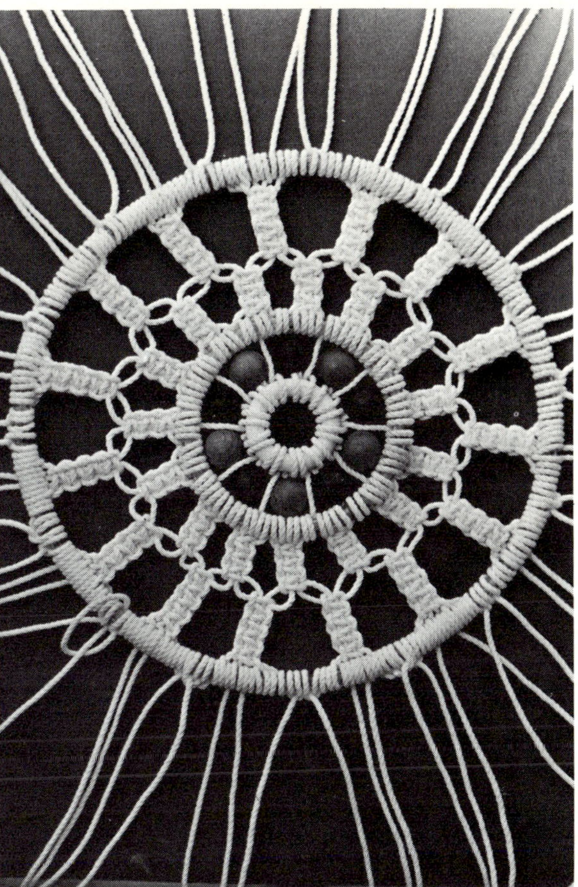

Further half hitches are worked to cover the ring. One half hitch is being worked in the bottom left hand side of the photograph.

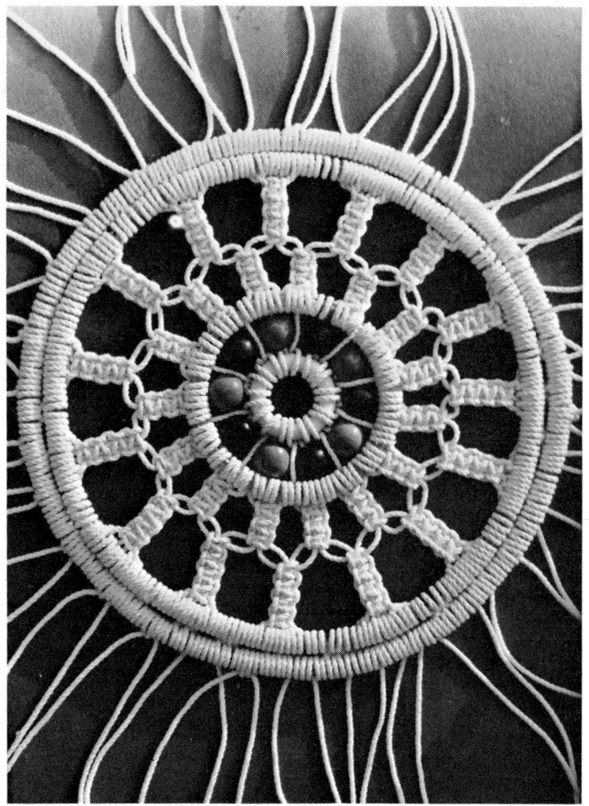

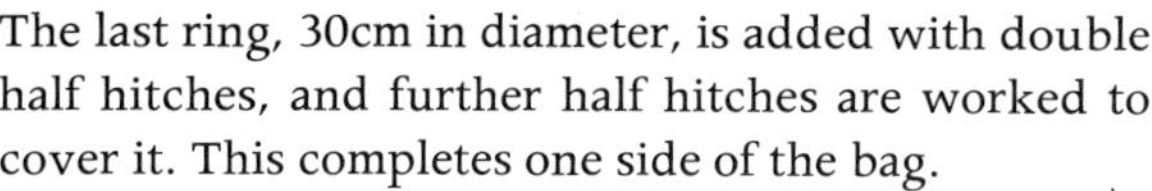

The last ring, 30cm in diameter, is added with double half hitches, and further half hitches are worked to cover it. This completes one side of the bag.

A second side must then be worked exactly the same.

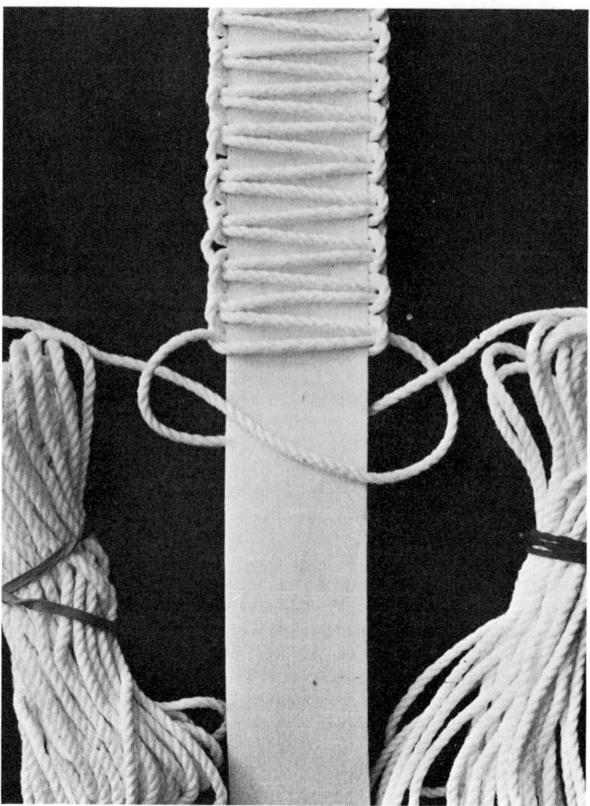

To make the gusset, which also forms the shoulder strap, work square knots along a 160cm piece of white belting. Join this length to form a circle.

The two completed sides are tied firmly to the circular piece, leaving the top of the bag open for a length of approximately 25cm.

Finally, the bag can be lined if required.

Jewelled evening cap with fringe and tassel

Child's towelling bikini decorated with fringe

Detail of macramé decoration on an evening dress

Full view of decorated evening dress

ROULEAU STRIPS IN MACRAMÉ

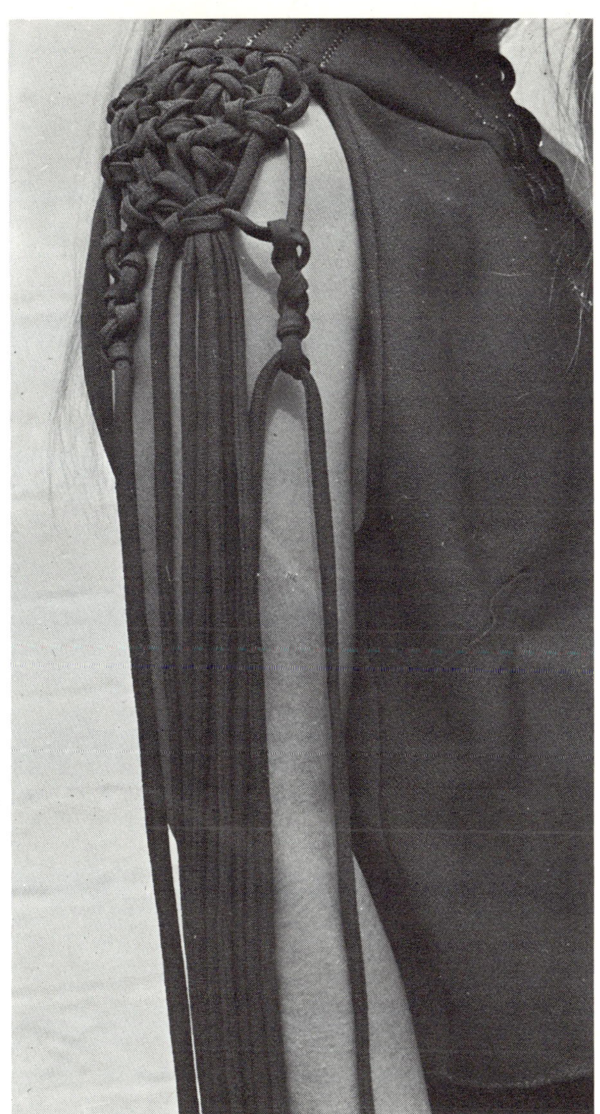

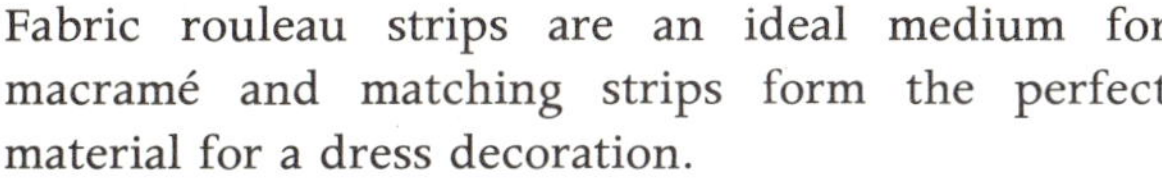

Fabric rouleau strips are an ideal medium for macramé and matching strips form the perfect material for a dress decoration.

The tunic sleeve trim *(above)* was made of rouleau strips of the same fabric as the dress. Square and half hitch knots were used.

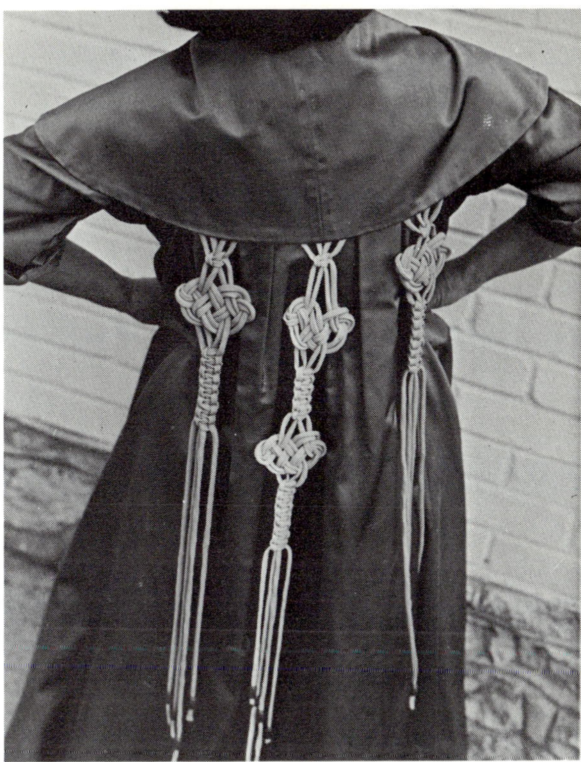

The evening coat *(above)* shows an added hanging from the collar shape made in rouleau strips. A large decorative knot and handmade clay beads are added at intervals down the hanging rouleaus.

Numerous knotted decorations could be used on this theme.

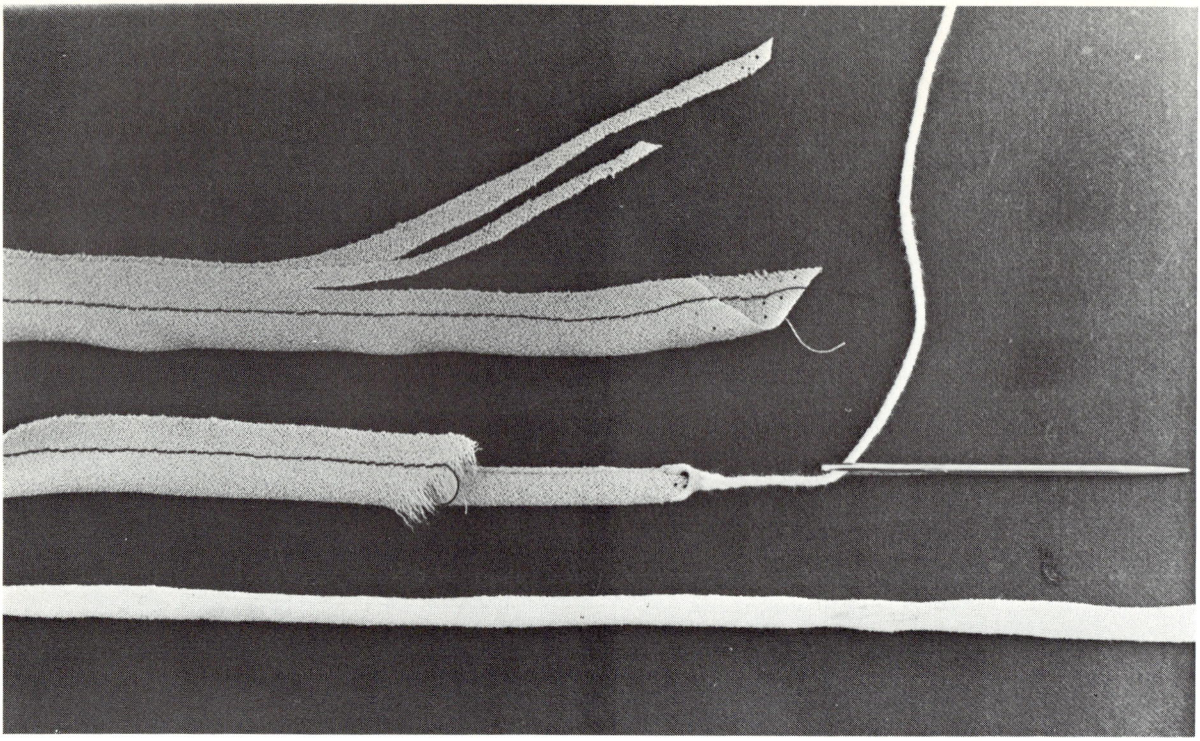

The rouleau is made by cutting strips of fabric on the bias approximately 7cm wide. The fabric is folded in half lengthwise with right sides together. The strip is machined along the centre, giving the desired width of rouleau between the folded edge of fabric and the row of machining. The surplus fabric is then trimmed away. The turning left should just fill the tube.

To draw the rouleau fabric through to the right side, thread a large bodkin with strong thread and attach firmly to one end of the fabric. Thread the bodkin through the inside of the tube. Draw through carefully until the right side of the fabric is showing. The photograph also shows the completed length of rouleau.

This photograph illustrates the completed knot worked in double thicknesses of rouleaus with a run of square knots above and below. This is a closeup of the knot used on the evening coat and shown step by step on the following page.

These four photographs show the working of a decorative knot which could be used in conjunction with the basic macramé knots. Double cords are used, and two colours help to distinguish the cords. Note the use of glass headed pins to hold the cords.

This is the knot used on the evening coat.

LUPÉ KNOT BELT

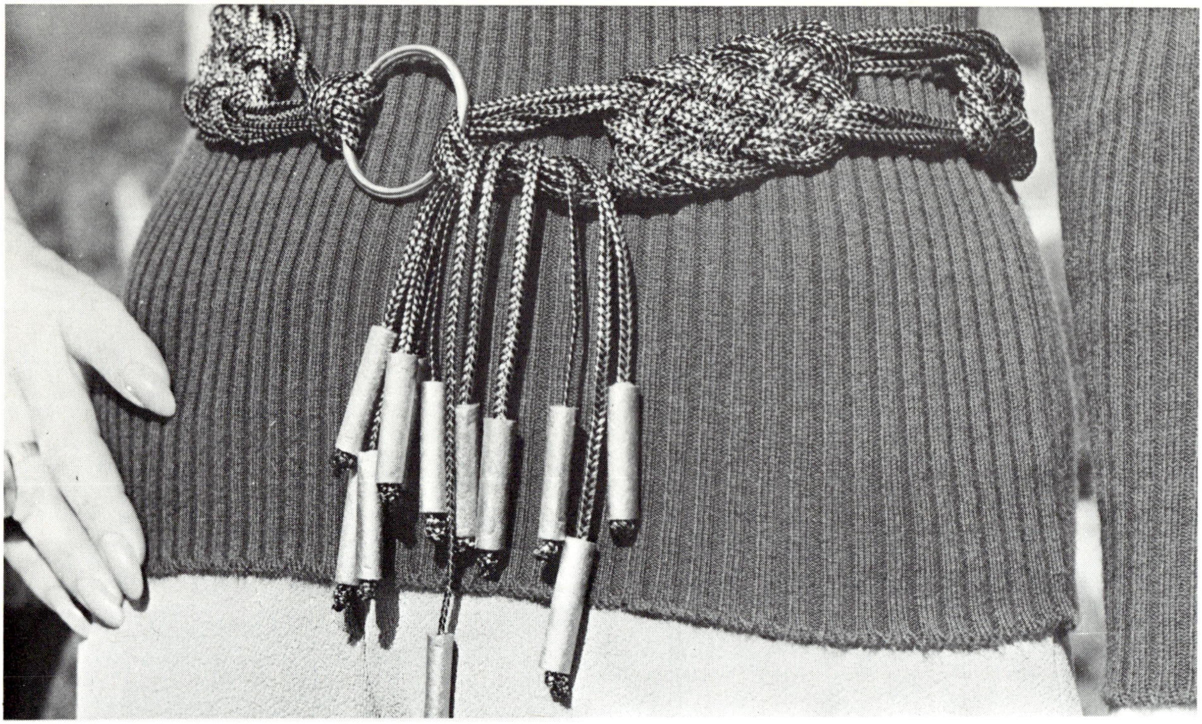

A more complicated but extremely attractive belt can be made from the lupé knot. Piping cord can be used but a sophisticated effect can be achieved by using more interesting materials. Six strands of gold and black Russia braid were used in the example shown *(above)*. A brass ring was used as a foundation and forms the fastening.

Alternative decorative knots such as those illustrated could also be used for making this belt. All can be incorporated with the basic macramé knots and add variety to the traditional type of knotting. Cords may be used singly or in pairs, or in groups of three or more like the lupé belt illustrated.

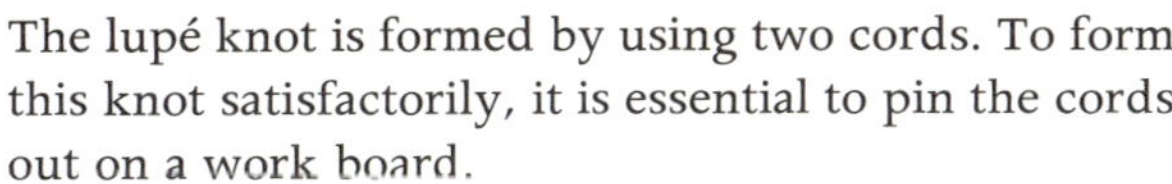

The lupé knot is formed by using two cords. To form this knot satisfactorily, it is essential to pin the cords out on a work board.

Pin out the first cord as illustrated. This shape, made with the first cord, is recognisable throughout the process.

1

Introduce the second cord.

The following seven photographs, starting with the one on the left, show the progression of the second cord 'over and under' the first cord.

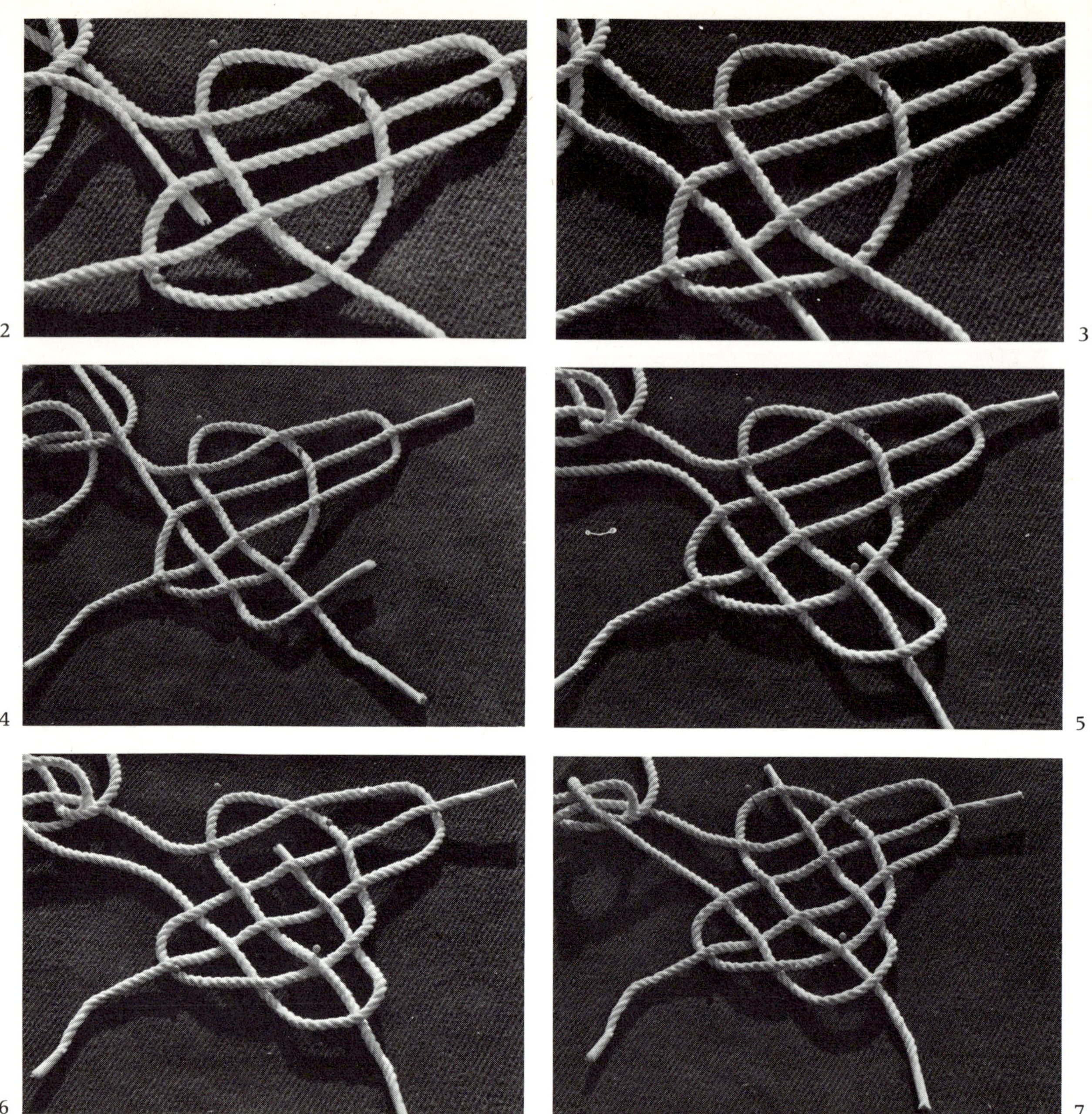
2 3 4 5 6 7

The working of the knot is complete. It is now necessary to adjust the lie of the cords in the knot so that they form an even pattern.

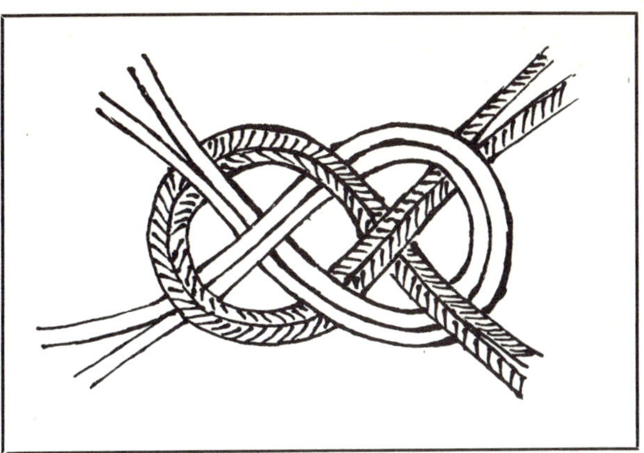

A Josephine knot is similar to the lupé knot but simpler to work. It could be used here in place of the lupé knot.

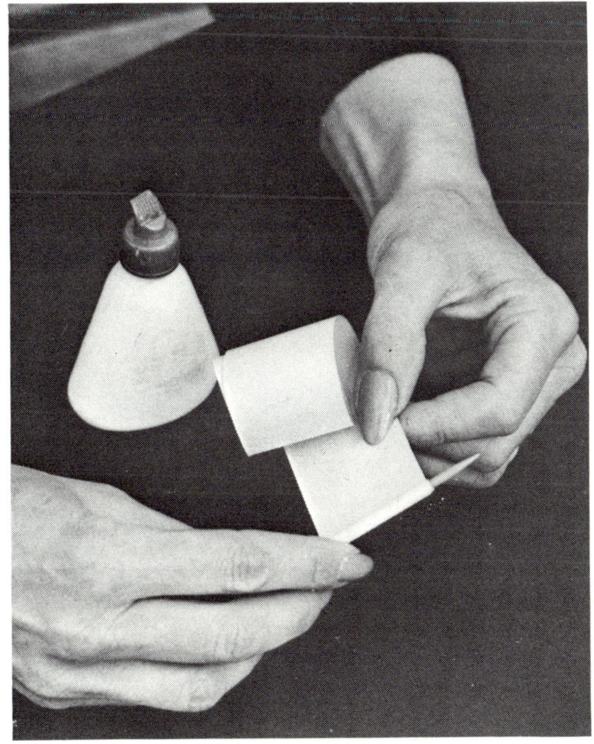

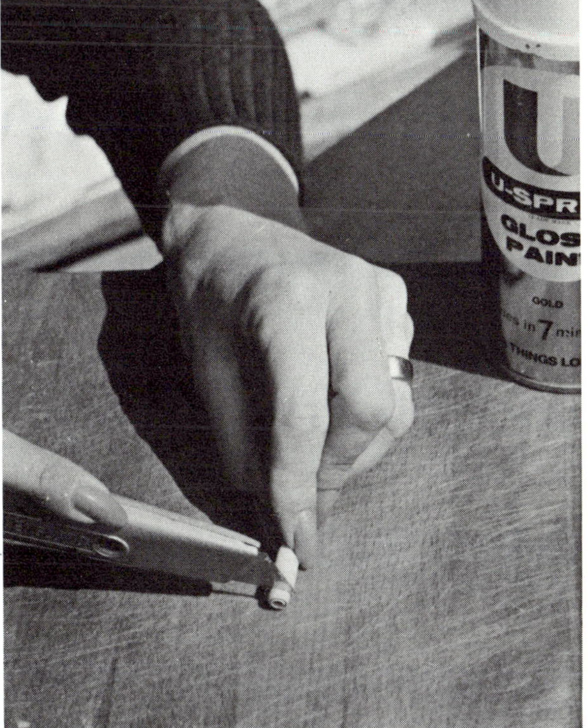

On the belt illustrated, six complete lupé knots were worked and the end cords were neatened with a bead. These beads were made by rolling a strip of lining paper round a knitting needle. Each bead was glued to secure the cut end of paper, trimmed, and sprayed with gold lacquer. The end of the tie cords were threaded through the beads and an overhand knot was tied to keep them in place.

INSERTIONS AND BRAIDS

The trousers *(right)* show an insertion, not a braid added after the trousers are made. Some means of attachment, such as cord ends, must therefore be left for sewing to the fabric. A thin fabric lining may be necessary to fit inside the trousers.

The photograph illustrates the example to be demonstrated step by step.

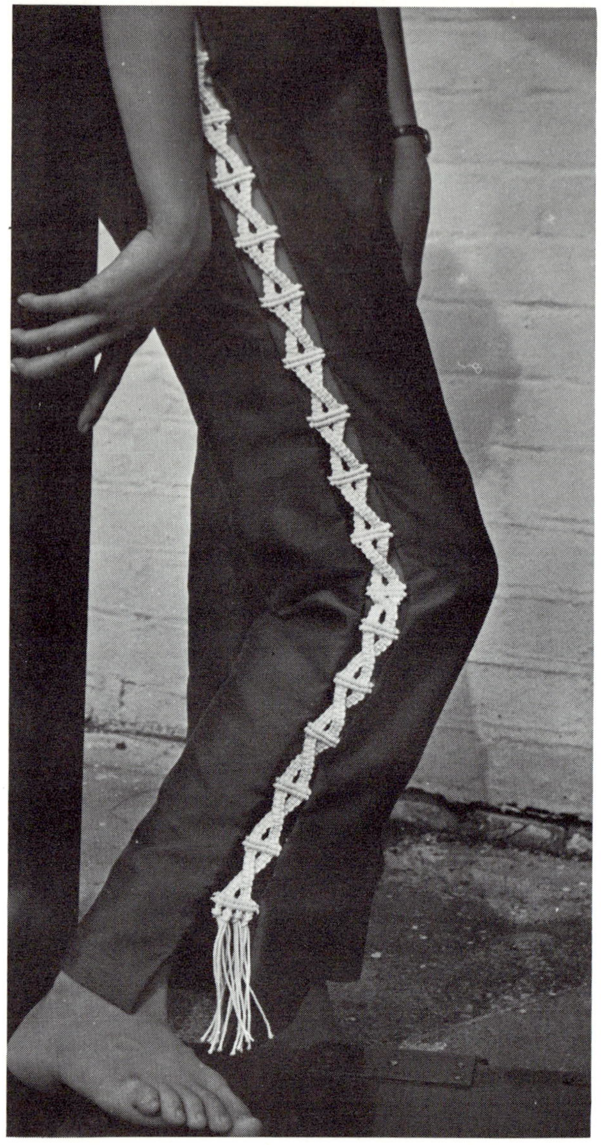

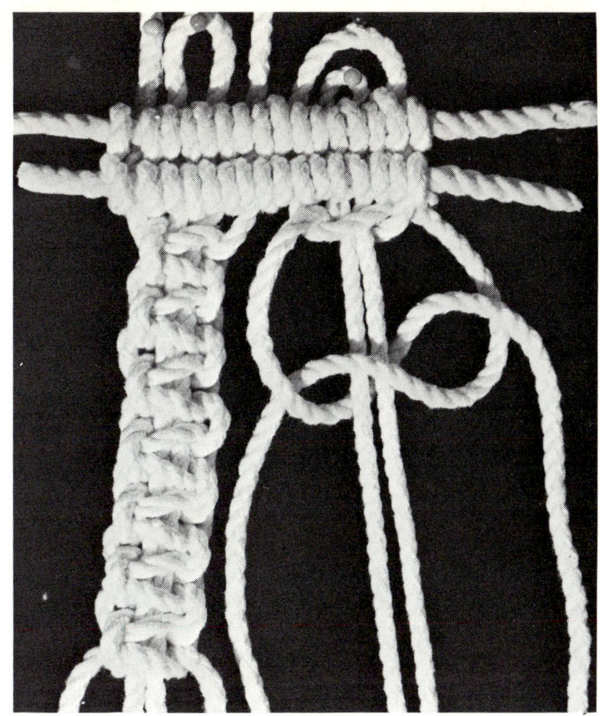

This photograph demonstrates the start of the insertion. Four cords are attached with a double half hitch knot to a short foundation cord. Each length is folded back and a second double half hitch is worked. This gives eight working cord lengths. A second short leader is introduced and double half hitches are worked across. Two runs are then made of an equal number of square knots.

The two lengths of square knots are then crossed over and a new leader introduced for cording with double half hitches. A second short leader is ready in place.

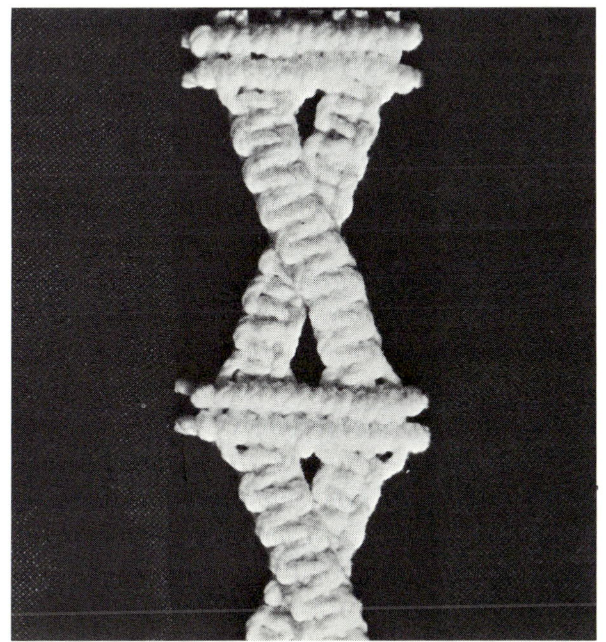

The square knots and cording are repeated throughout for the desired insertion length.

A detail of the insertion. The ends of the short leaders form the cords to be sewn to the fabric.

THREE BRAIDS OR TRIMS

These trims are formed by knotting which could be used for the illustrations on pages 84-6. They would be worked separately and sewn to the garment with tiny stitches.

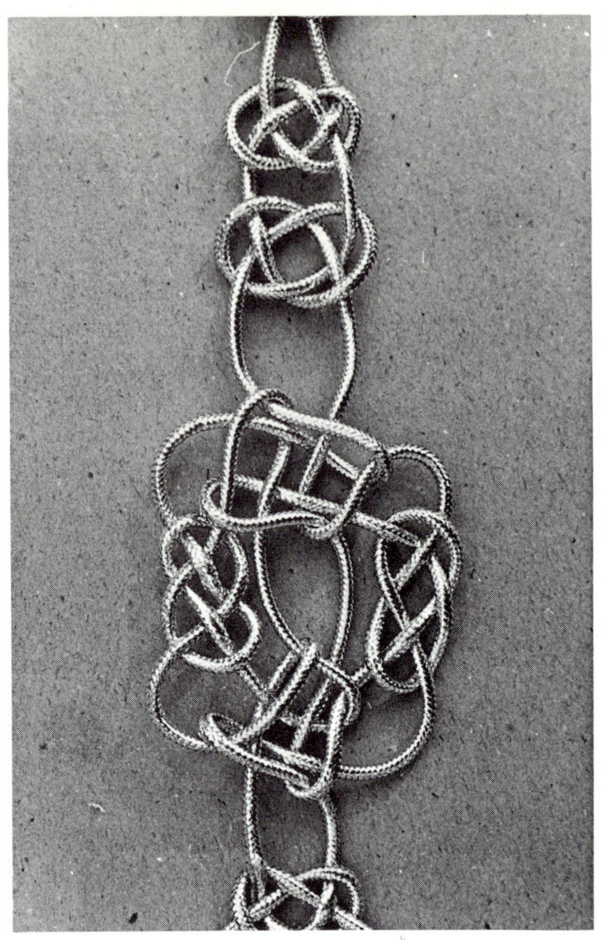

a. Two knots form this decoration: the four part crown butterfly knot and the Josephine knot.

b. A type of basket weave knot.

c. A type of plaiting in piping cord with a firmer cord running straight through the braid.

WOOL BRAIDS

a. b.

a. Simple square knot braid with picots on opposite sides. Two colours of thick rug wool were used for this braid.

b. Similar to *a.* but the picots are diagonally opposite.

c. d.

c. Rug wool braid worked with two half hitches over two centre cords, working two half hitches from each side. Two colours are used for this braid.

d. Similar to *c.* but three half hitches are worked from each side over two centre cords. Black and gold cords are used for this braid.

Ideas for using wool braids on sleeves, skirts and as a bodice trim.

Braided jacket with possible ideas for the trouser decoration.

Ideas for using braids or insertions.

A GOLD MACRAMÉ BODICE

Evening dresses lend themselves to the use of macramé in many ways. The dress illustrated *(above)* is made in white polyester crêpe; it is fairly loose fitting, with a kimono sleeve and a draped, slightly gathered skirt. The bodice is tight fitting under the bustline. This shape was used as the basic pattern for the macramé. A gold cord of mixed lurex and matt yarn is used for the work, and large handmade gold clay beads with dull wooden gold beads were added to the cords during the knotting process. The raw ends of the cord were secured in the seams of the dress as these were machined together.

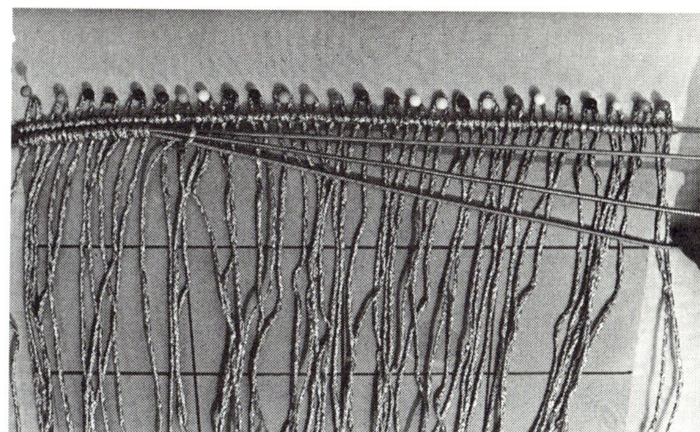

The photograph illustrates the start of this piece of work. The paper shape of the dress pattern piece is pinned to the padded work board and the dark lines are drawn as guides to keep the knotting in straight lines. A small loop is left at the top of the work, held in place with a pin, before working the first row of double half hitches to form a row of cording. Here, the second row of double half hitches is being worked over three thicknesses of cord to make a thicker row of cording.

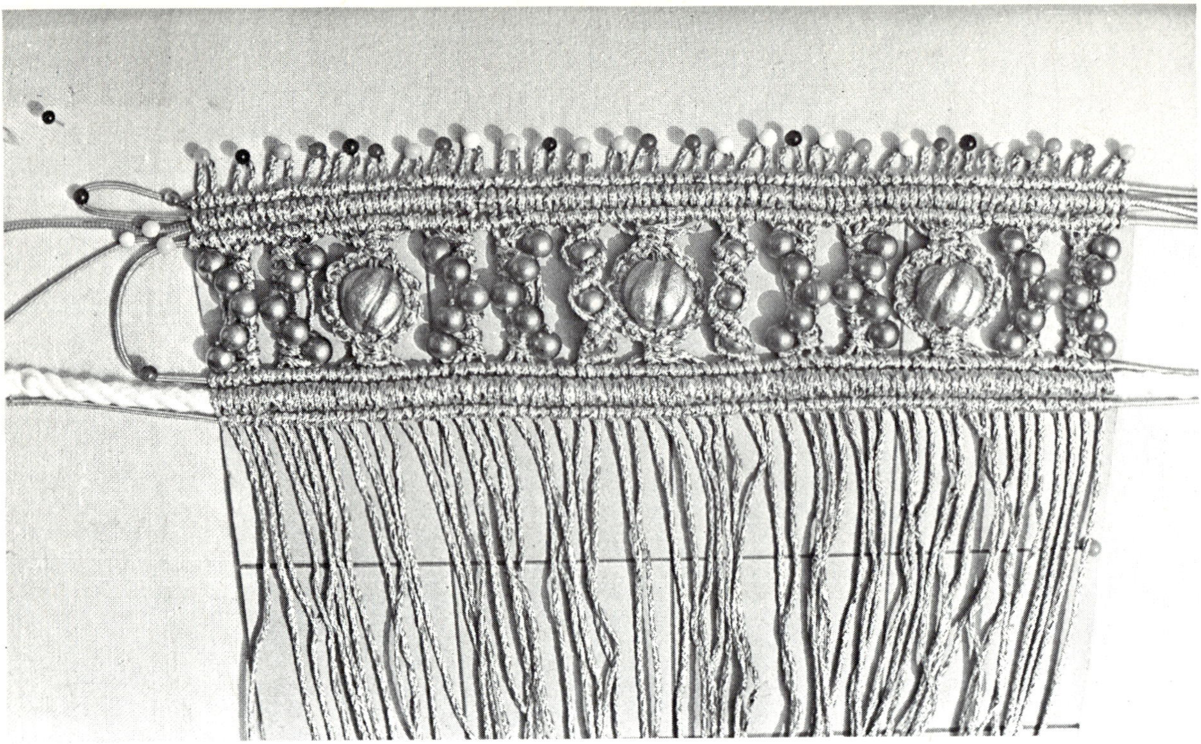

The first completed pattern is now finished. It can be seen that three rows of cording were worked at the top before the beaded pattern was started. The photograph below shows a closeup of this pattern. This beaded pattern is then followed by three more rows of cording: one thin row, one thicker row, and the third row the same thickness as the first row.

Clay beads can be handmade and painted as described and illustrated on page 40.

The closeup of the beaded pattern illustrates a cross of beads, formed with double half hitches using a bead on each loop. The half hitch is first passed over three cords, then two cords, and finally one cord in the centre to form the diagonal line of the cross into the centre. The process is then reversed to bring the line of beads out again. This is repeated in the opposite way for the second side of the cross.

The large bead is placed on the centre cords of a square knot run with reversed double half hitches running on either side.

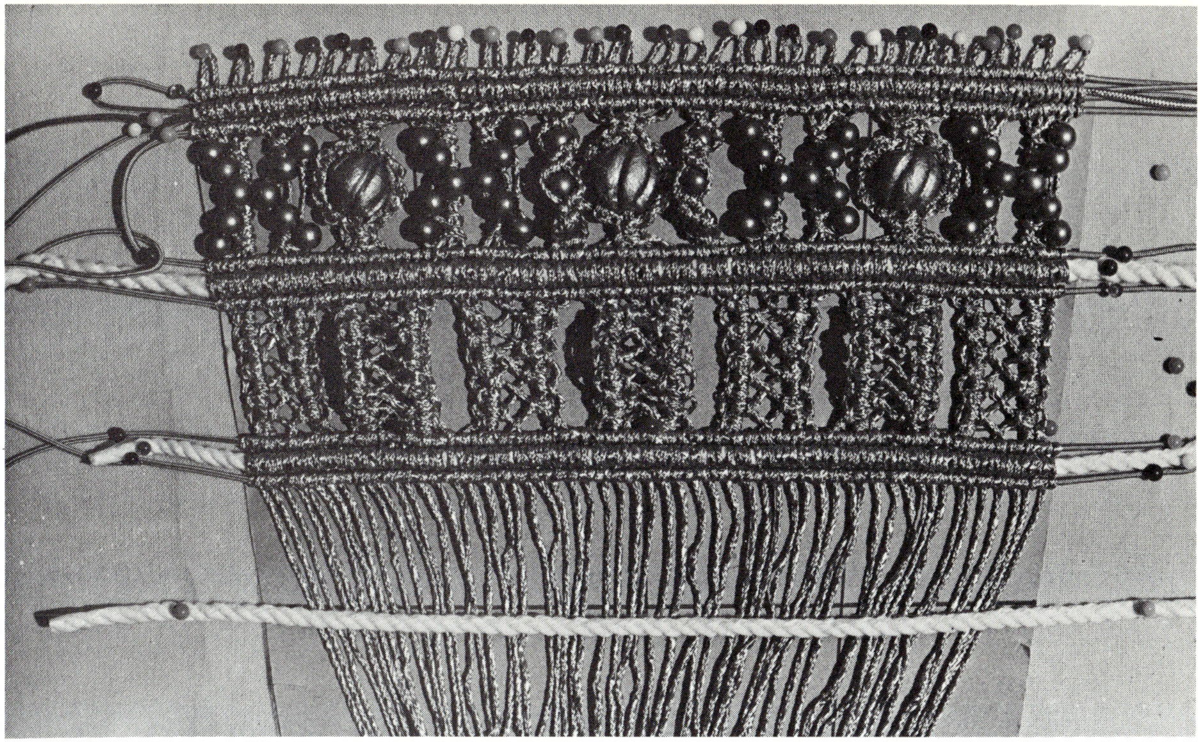

This photograph illustrates the second pattern row in the design which is formed from different lengths of braid. The braid is made in a criss cross design with reversible double half hitches. The different lengths are secured to the leaders of the next row of cording, allowing some lengths to bulge out away from the work.

This is the completed piece of work.

FRINGES

Macramé is derived from an Arabic word which signifies an ornamental fringe and, indeed, most effective dress fringes can be made. Various materials can be used and beads added to emphasise the design.

White silk fringing has been used on this coloured bikini.

A child's beach outfit made in printed towelling with a simple cotton fringe. Two rows of cording and overhand knots twisting the threads give a crossed effect.

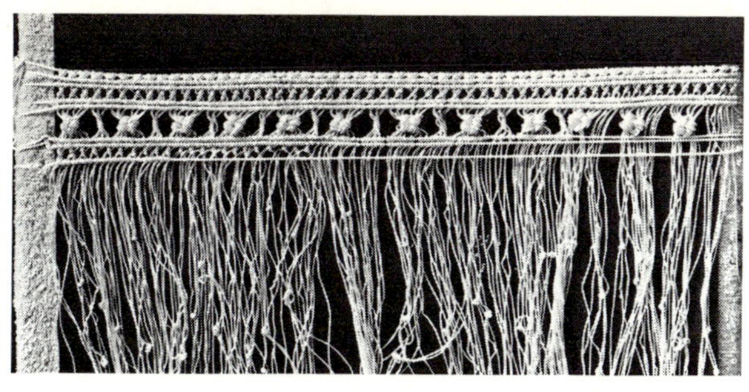

The fringe for a large area should ideally be worked in one piece. When making the fringe for the bikini illustrated opposite, a length of 100cm was required. A large board is covered with a towel and the required length of cord for the total fringe length is anchored as a foundation cord. The working cords are then attached and the knotting started.

In the photograph, various stages are shown: horizontal cording, vertical cording, then horizontal cording followed by a Chinese crown knot (as illustrated on page 33). More cording is then worked before the working cords are left free for the fringe.

This shows the detail of the fringe.

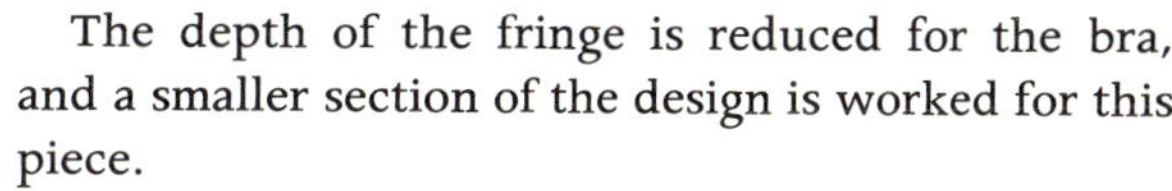

The depth of the fringe is reduced for the bra, and a smaller section of the design is worked for this piece.

Rug wool, and many other types of knitting yarn, make excellent macramé fringes. Rug wool is used for these two fringes:

This simple fringe comprises a foundation cord with a row of reversed double half hitches and two rows of cording.

A braid is first made with even picots on either side for this fringe. The picots give a loop for securing the fringe cords with a reversed double half hitch.

Fringe made in a fine purple rayon knitted yarn with cording and tassels. Matt purple wood beads are used at intervals. The fringe forms a trim to a pair of evening slacks.

Another fringe trim made in crysette cotton.

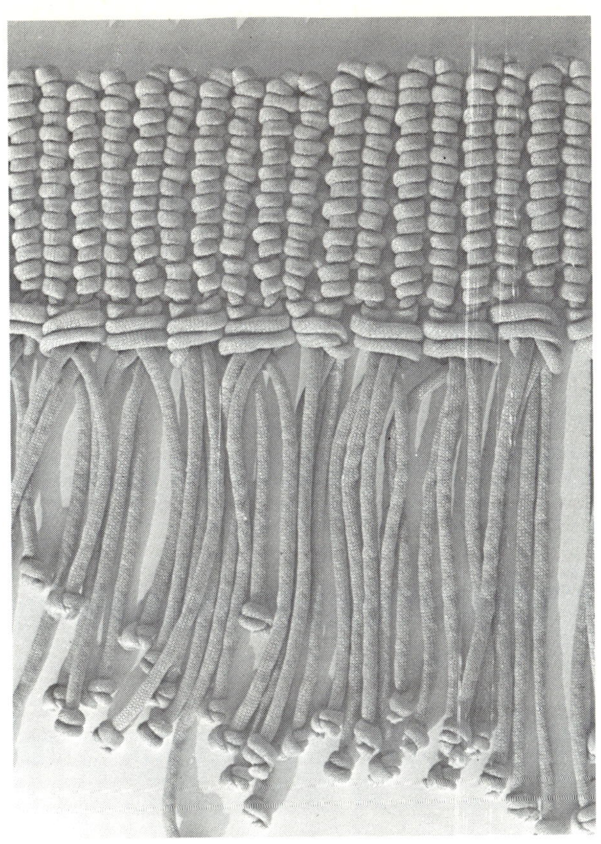

a. Vertical cording forms this fringe, which is made in tubular rayon yarn. A looped fringe is added to one edge of the cording.

b. A twisted rayon mercerised yarn is used for this traditional-design braid.

c. A similar fringe to the one above.

Fringes used as a trim for scarves and stoles.

Further uses of fringes: as a trim, and forming a complete skirt.

MORE FRINGES

LEATHER JERKIN FRINGE

This leather jerkin is made of green calf leather with a black fringe. A scallop edged heading is used, and shiny black beads with a deep tasselled fringe.

The photograph shows the fringe in detail. The foundation cord is made the required length for the hem of the jerkin, ie 90cm. The scallops are worked (details on the next page), followed by two rows of cording. Beads are placed on every sixth cord and six single half hitches are worked over the five cords between the beads. Three more rows of cording follow the beads. The photographs on the following pages demonstrate the making of the fringe and tassels.

MAKING THE SCALLOPS

Three cords are doubled on to a foundation cord. Note that two cords hang down and one cord is placed upwards.

Reversed double half hitches are worked on the cords placed upwards; five in all. The cords are then anchored to the foundation cord with a double half hitch.

The second cord is anchored to the foundation cord with a double half hitch.

For the fringe illustrated on the jerkin, a new leader is introduced and two rows of cording are worked.

MAKING THE CORDING AND TASSELLED FRINGE

Two colours are used to demonstrate the changing positions of the cords *(Above left and right)*.

When the rows of horizontal cording are completed, the diagonal design is started. Four rows are worked over six cords (this can be decreased to four or increased to eight or more). To join the blocks together, take the last leader from the left hand block and continue to work double half hitches with the cords from the right hand block, keeping the leader in the same direction. To complete the lower left hand block, take the last leader from the top right hand block and continue to work double half hitches to the left; follow the direction of the last row of cording from the top right hand block. Work four rows of cording on each block.

The tassels are made when all the cording is complete. Note that the tassel is placed by joining the lower points of the diagonal cording. Take all the working cords and tie an overhand knot.

To illustrate more clearly, a darker cord is now added to give extra lengths of cord in the tassel. These are placed over the overhand knot.

To secure the cords, use a small blob of rubber based adhesive. Then take one piece of working cord and wrap it round all the other cords with a half hitch. Note the use of a 'sling'. A sling is a separate piece of cord which is doubled, the looped end being placed towards the head of the tassel before securing the tassel with the half hitch.

Taking the cord which made the half hitch, twist it tightly around all the cords, including the sling, several times. Place the end of the cord through the sling and draw downwards to tighten.

OTHER IDEAS FOR USING A FRINGE

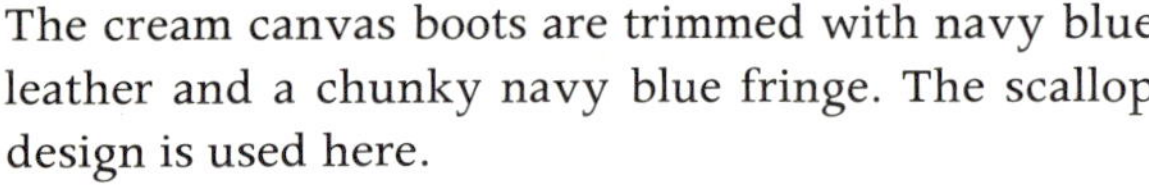

The cream canvas boots are trimmed with navy blue leather and a chunky navy blue fringe. The scallop design is used here.

A jewelled evening hat with a hanging fringe and centre tassel.

USEFUL TIPS

ESTIMATING LENGTH OF CORD

While it is possible to join threads during the working of a project, it is preferable to use one length of material where possible, and it is therefore important to estimate the required length. The design and the type of knots used control the quantity of material required, but the rule of thumb guide is that four or five times the finished length is sufficient. This must be doubled if the thread is being attached by a looped knot. If the piece of working thread is very long an elastic band is used to hold the cords during work.

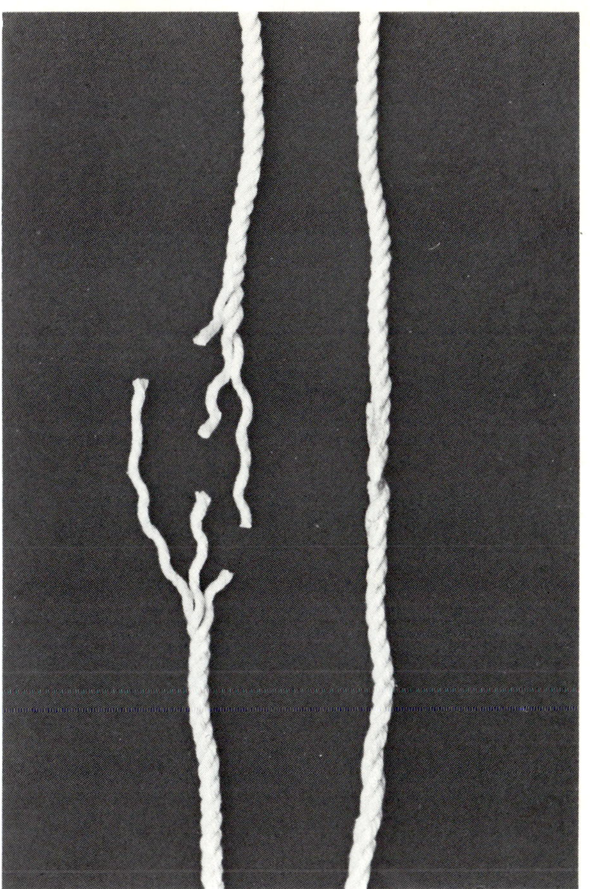

JOINING THREADS

If you run out of thread during the project, more thread can be added. With single ply cords, a join can be made by sewing together the cut ends of the short length and the new piece of thread. If the join can be arranged in an inconspicuous area of the design, an ordinary joining knot can be used and placed on the wrong side of the work.

With threads that consist of two or more plys, a neater join can be made by cutting the ends to different lengths and sticking together with rubber based adhesive.

The photograph *(Right)* illustrates this type of join.

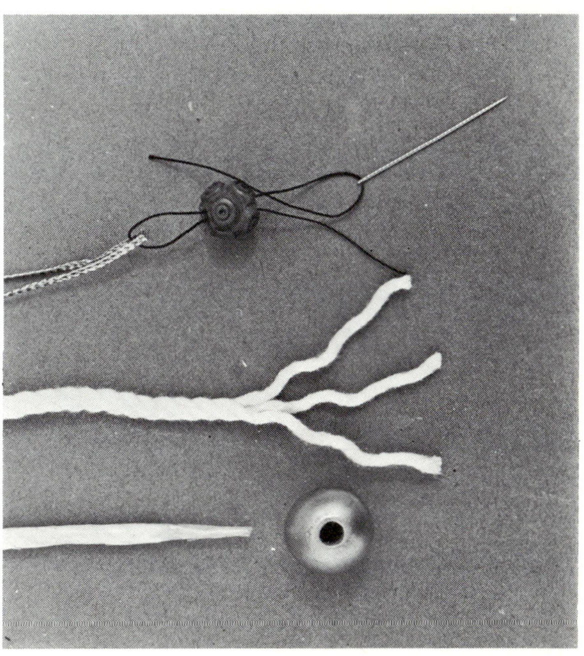

THREADING BEADS

Wood beads which are recommended for macramé work usually have large threading holes. If the thread becomes unravelled, adhesive tape placed round the cut ends helps to make a point for easy threading.

A 'sling' is helpful. A fine needle, threaded with strong thin thread, is placed through the bead and returned back again to form a loop. Place the macramé yarn through this loop and pull the threads back through the bead. The photograph *(Right)* illustrates both methods of threading beads.

ADDING NEW THREADS DURING WORK

New threads can be added quite easily during the knotting processes. When working in square knots, double or single cords may be added by looping the new lengths through the working cords.

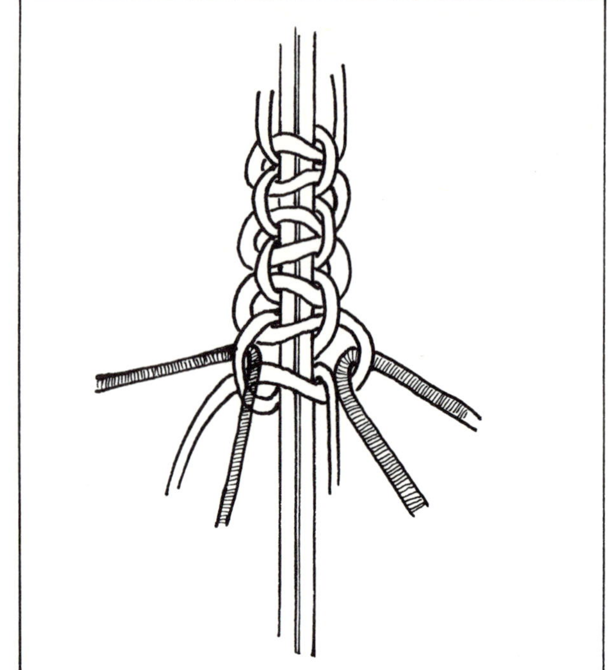

a. A cord being looped into each side of a square knot.

b. Two cords being looped into a square knot fabric. To increase when cording: the new threads can be added to the leader by working a reversed double half hitch with the new cord.

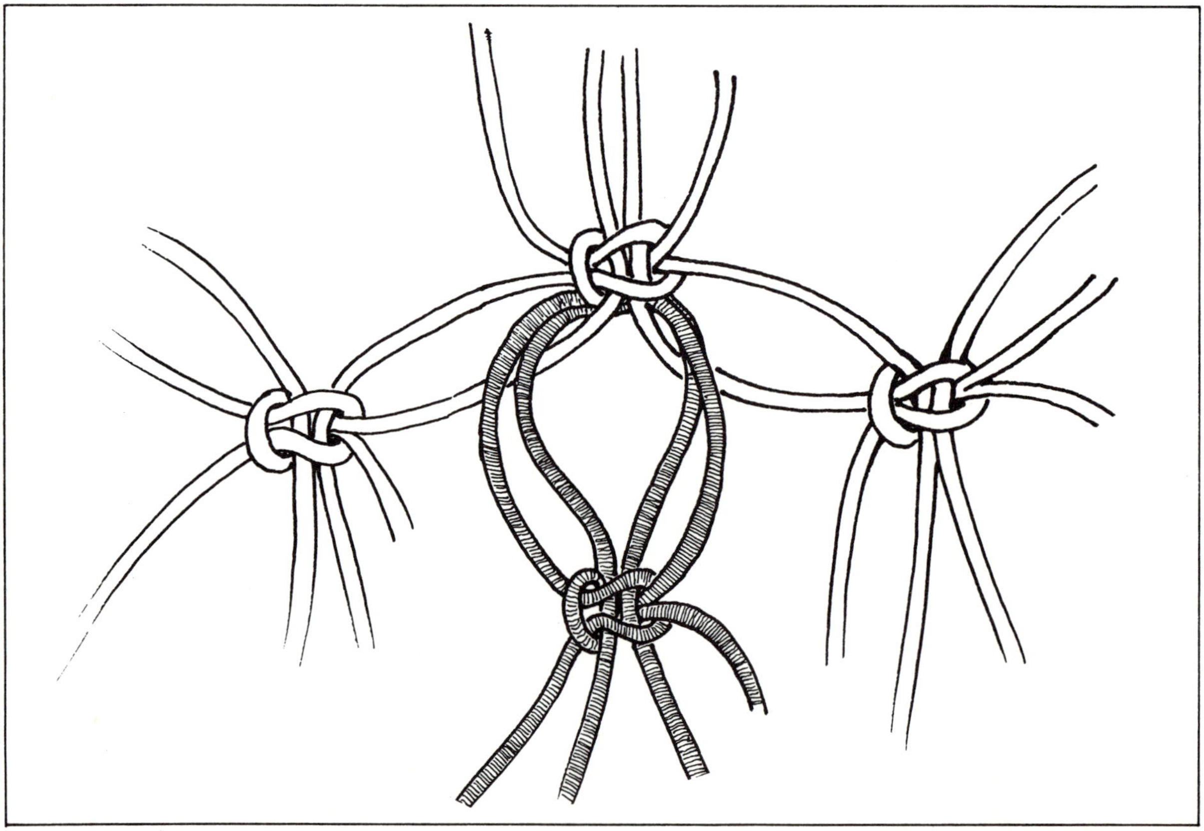

DYEING YOUR MATERIALS

Read the manufacturer's instructions before starting to dye any material.

All threads to be dyed should be washed first. Test a piece of thread before dyeing the complete supply to obtain the correct colour shade. If using water dyes, care must be taken to ensure that all the dye is dissolved before placing the threads into the liquid. If large quantities of thread are to be dyed, it should be wound into a skein and very loosely tied before immersion.

PAPER PATTERNS

When making a macramé bodice top, shaped neckline, or a flared skirt section, a paper pattern may be used to provide an accurate outline. The paper pattern is tacked to the work pad and the cords are secured with pins along the seam line. The knotting is then worked across the shape, tying in new cords as the pattern develops. Alternatively, the spaces between the knots can be increased very slightly to give an increase in size or reduced very slightly to give a decrease.

TO GIVE A FIRM EDGE TO A PATTERN PIECE

The cord being used for the macramé can be plaited (three pieces) to give an outline, and the macramé threads can be knotted into the loops of the plaiting at intervals.

UNDOING KNOTS

The knots used in macramé work usually lock fairly tightly, but with the help of a small fid or other blunt pointed instrument (the pointed ivory tool, 5cm long, in the upper photograph on page 8) the knots can be prised open.

CONTROLLING LARGE DECORATIVE KNOTS

Large knots, when made in certain materials, sometimes slip out of line. To prevent this happening, the materials can be lightly caught on the wrong side with small sewing stitches or a small blob of adhesive.

USING A CROCHET HOOK

When working cording knots over a ring, it becomes difficult towards the end of the process to place the cords through the ring. A crochet hook is useful for drawing the cords through accurately, as illustrated on page 55.

USING A SLING

A sling is used to secure the working thread firmly when tying the head of a tassel, as illustrated on page 99.

FURTHER READING

Harvey, Virginia. *Macramé: the Art of Creative Knotting,* Van Nostrand, New York, 1967

Harvey, Virginia. *Color and Design*, Van Nostrand, New York, 1967

Short, Eirian. *Introducing Macramé*, Batsford, London, 1970

Ashley, Clifford. *The Ashley Book of Knots*, Doubleday, New York, 1944 and 1960

de Dillmont, Thérèse. *The Encyclopaedia of Needlework*, first published in the late 1800s, original edition obtainable from secondhand bookshops.

LIST OF SUPPLIERS

A search in hardware shops, marine suppliers, wool shops, weavers' suppliers, Government surplus stores, hobby shops, and needlecraft shops should produce a variety of materials with which to knot. Sewing departments of large stores stock many different kinds of thread. Here is a list of suppliers in Great Britain:

Arthur Beale, 194 Shaftesbury Avenue, London WC2 (strings and cords)

Branches of multiple stores such as John Lewis and Debenhams

Dryad Ltd, Northgates, Leicester (wide selection of craft materials)

Ells & Farrier Ltd, 5 Princes Street, London W1 (beads)

Mace & Nairn, 89 Crane Street, Salisbury, Wiltshire (metallic threads, twists, and cords)

Nottingham Handicraft Co Ltd, Melton Road, West Bridgford, Nottingham (wide selection of materials)

The Hobby Horse, 15-17 Langton Street, London SW10 (send 15p for catalogue of macramé materials)

The Needlewoman Shop, 146-148 Regent Street, London W1 (large range of threads)